LETTING PHOTOS SPEAK

LETTING PHOTOS SPEAK

VISIO DIVINA AND OTHER APPROACHES TO CONTEMPLATIVE PHOTOGRAPHY

Stephen J. Radley, Philip J. Richter and Andy J. Lindley

DARTON · LONGMAN + TODD

First published in 2023 by
Darton, Longman and Todd Ltd
1 Spencer Court
140 – 142 Wandsworth High Street
London SW18 4JJ

ISBN: 978-1-915412-12-6

A catalogue record for this book is available from the British Library.

Printed and bound in Great Britain by Bell & Bain, Glasgow

CONTENTS

List of images and illustrations   7

Chapter 1: Introduction – contemplation, mindfulness and wellbeing   9

    Contemplation and mindfulness   12

    Wellbeing   18

    Photography and wellbeing – personal accounts   21

    From war to wonder – Steve Radley   21

    From Fleet Street to landscape – Paul Sanders   23

Chapter 2: Exploring meanings in photos – from theological refection to *visio divina*   25

    Illustrative approach   25

    Discovery approach   27

    Visio divina   33

    Extended example – Tim Mooney's *visio divina* process   40

    Visio divina in practice   42

Chapter 3: Letting photos speak to us   45

    Placing the present in the context of the past   46

    Re-encountering places and moments of spiritual significance through your standout images   54

    Revealing patterns of change in the light of constancy   58

Symbolising life's choices and enabling reflection on your choices   64

Revealing colour and expressing emotion   69

Finding beauty in the ordinary   74

Connecting with others — stories secular and sacred   81

The power of photos to meet us where we are   85

Chapter 4: Letting photos speak in groups   86

Why a group?   86

Photos as a third conversation partner   89

A practical example: Divine Focus   91

The Divine Focus Gathering   93

Workshops   94

Using photos in more traditional worship   96

Chapter 5: Building a personal photo journal — a modern 'Book of Hours'   99

Worked example of how our templates can be used   103

Templates   109

Bookmark overlays   131

Over to you …   136

Notes   137

LIST OF IMAGES AND ILLUSTRATIONS

Chapter 1

Illustration 1. Venn Diagram — Mindfulness and Contemplation   14

Chapter 2

Illustrative Approach

Image 1. Italian Sunday Market © Philip Richter   26

Visio divina in practice

Image 2. 'Migrant Mother', by Dorothea Lange 1936, Library of Congress,   42
Prints and Photographs Division, FSA/OWI Collection (Public Domain)

Chapter 3

Placing the present in the context of the past

Image 3. The Sycamore Tree © Andy Lindley   47

Re-encountering places and moments of spiritual significance through your standout images

Image 4. Night Sky on Harter Fell © Stephen Radley   55

Revealing patterns of change in the light of constancy

Image 5. Swift Exit © Stephen Radley   59

Finding beauty in the ordinary

Image 6. War Graves © Andy Lindley   74

Connecting with others — stories secular and sacred

Image 7. Dandelion Clock © Stephen Radley   81

Chapter 4

Why a group?
Image 8. Wooden Drawers © Andy Lindley   87

A practical example: Divine Focus
Image 9. Joy © Andy Lindley   92

Chapter 5

A modern 'Book of Hours'
Image 10. Book of Hours, Simon Bening (Netherlandish) ca. 1530–35,   100
Metropolitan Museum of Art, accession number 2015.706 (Public Domain)

Worked example
Image 11. Time Stands Still – St Pierre Basilica, Avignon © Philip Richter   107

Over to you…
Image 12. Entertaining Angels Unawares © Stephen Radley   135

CHAPTER 1

Introduction – contemplation, mindfulness and wellbeing

In one of his blogs, the American photographer and author, David duChemin, recalls an incident he witnessed when on holiday in Venice. He saw a man carrying a heavy tripod and camera turn to a friend and, pointing to the crowd who were taking photographs with their phone cameras, sneer and say, 'Now everybody thinks they are a photographer'. Reflecting on this incident, duChemin's initial thought is a question: Why should this matter? Reflecting further, he supposes the man learnt his craft when there was a certain mystique surrounding photography. Cameras were expensive and necessitated saving to own one; film was costly and had to be handled carefully. There was a technical knowledge required to set the camera to ensure the film was exposed properly to create a good image. It was then necessary to mix chemicals at critically exact temperatures to develop the negative and then a further process involving more chemicals to produce a positive print ready to be viewed.

DuChemin supposes for those who spent a long time mastering this craft the title 'photographer' can conjure up something of importance, a badge of honour which can easily become what he calls, a 'golden calf' – a reference to a biblical story in which people idolised a golden image in place of the true God.[1] The mass adoption and accessibility of the craft of photography makes the title 'photographer' less important than it perhaps was historically; and he speculates that photography was really about the ego for people like this man in Venice. He sees this as unfortunate, as he claims the real purpose behind photography is not the self, but rather 'a way of seeing the world and being more alive to the world … The more of us that have our eyes opened, the better.'[2]

This book is co-authored by three friends, brought together by a common interest in photography and its potential to benefit the world in which we live, our relationships and our wellbeing through the way it can help us see and experience the world. Like duChemin, we believe photography can be an eye opener, helping us to see the beauty of the world in new ways, but we also believe photography can be deeply spiritual. By this, we mean it can help us reflect on the world, our place within the world, and what it means to be alive. If you want to explore the spirituality of photography further, then Philip's earlier book, *Spirituality in Photography*, is worth reading.[3]

The pages that follow have found their expression jointly between us, but we will each bring in some of our own stories. We hope this will help personalise the book and place what we write practically. Our understanding of contemplative photography comes from our own practice and ministry and our lived experience of photography's benefit to our own spiritual and mental wellbeing. We share practices and insights we have found personally helpful and exercises we have used with others in churches, photography retreats and workshops we have led. As such, we do not share theoretical ideas, but things that have been tested and found to be of benefit by both us and others alongside whom we have worked.

As authors we each find our spiritual understanding of life is founded in a Christian tradition. We believe that photography has the potential to make accessible to everyone a couple of ancient Christian contemplative tools called *visio divina* and the Book of Hours. In the UK these practices can be traced back to the monastic tradition and it was through monasteries and convents that some of the UK's most important institutions were founded, for example, education and healthcare. Arguably, in these institutions we see the earliest UK examples of promoting what we now call 'wellbeing'.

Although as authors we come from a Christian tradition, our hope is that this book will be open and accessible to people of all faiths and none. Our book is framed by our tradition, but if we use a term which you find unhelpful, such as 'God' or 'prayer', we invite you to replace it with a word which has more meaning for you, perhaps 'otherness' or 'the unknown' or 'reflection'. We all experience the world in different ways; together, by respecting and sharing our differences, personal growth is enriched and deepened.

In the first chapter of this book, we will be exploring some of the interconnections between contemplation and mindfulness and the effects that photography can have on wellbeing, including some personal testimonies of how photography has helped individuals find healing from past hurts. In Chapter 2, we will outline some ways of exploring meanings in photos, ranging from theological reflection to *visio divina*. We will consider how photography can be a place of unrushed reflection or contemplation, involving the mind, emotions and body. In Chapter 3, we will be suggesting how you can best let photos speak to you. We will propose a number of practical exercises using photos to help us connect with ourselves, others, nature, and God. How, for instance, might we find beauty in the ordinary and even the apparently ugly? Chapter 4 moves on to look at how photos can be used in groups and we share some practical examples of how images can speak effectively in group contexts, including workshops and alternative styles of worship. Finally, in Chapter 5, we invite you to draw together your reflections in a personal photo journal, inspired by the ancient practice of keeping a 'Book of Hours'. It doesn't matter how you read our book — you can either read it as a whole or simply dip into the sections which interest you.

Caveat: some our exercises suggest focusing on your breathing. Some people find this difficult, and, if this is you, then please feel free to use a different anchor in your body, such as noticing the feel of your clothes on your skin or the weight of your body pushing down into your chair (if sitting) or through your feet (if standing). If you live with a mental health condition, we would always advise you speak with a health care practitioner before engaging in any contemplative or mindful practice.

Contemplation and mindfulness

Fundamentally, both contemplation and mindfulness call their practitioners into a stance of greater awareness of their bodies and emotions, and attention to how they are leading their lives. This attention is twofold: first, to the physical world, for instance, the weather, the people and items that surround us; secondly, to our inner world of thoughts, feelings and emotions.

Towards the end of his life, the Trappist monk Thomas Merton (1915-1968) explored the potential interplay between contemplation and photography. Reflecting on contemplation he said: 'Contemplation is the highest expression of man's intellectual and spiritual life. It is that life itself, fully awake, fully active, fully aware that it is alive. It is spontaneous awe at the sacredness of life, of being. It is gratitude for life, for awareness and for being. It is a vivid realization of the fact that life and being in us proceed from an invisible, transcendent and infinitely abundant Source. Contemplation is, above all, awareness of the reality of that Source. It knows the Source ...'[4] Naturally, if he were writing today, in all probability he would use more inclusive language.

Franciscan monk, Richard Rohr, who founded the Center for Action and Contemplation in New Mexico, states, 'The contemplative mind is about receiving and being present to the moment, to the now, without judgment, analysis, or critique. Contemplative "knowing" is a much more holistic, heart-centred knowing, where mind, heart, soul, and senses are open and receptive to the moment just as it is.'[5]

Both of these spiritual practitioners reassure us that we may never get good at contemplation, in fact Thomas Merton goes out of his way to say that if we think we are good at contemplating, we almost certainly are not and need to exercise some humility.

There is currently a growing body of research on mindfulness and especially the benefits of stilling one's mind and paying attention to the present moment. This is very similar to what contemplation invites us to do. Research into mindfulness has shown that it can literally rewire our brains and Christian mystics believe a similar, though more profound, process happens through Christian contemplation, which they envisage as remaining silently open to God's presence, so as to think with compassion, kindness, and a lack of attachment to our own desires.

This idea is reflected in the Hebrew Bible in the Book of Psalms, a collection of ancient hymns and poems compiled in or before the second-century BCE. The psalmist wrote: 'Be still and know that I am God. I am exalted among the nations. I am exalted in the earth. The Lord of hosts is with us; the God of Jacob is our refuge' (Psalm 46:10-11).

The idea of stillness is counter cultural today, in western culture which values and worships the god of busyness through our attention-grabbing economy. But, used sensitively, contemplative photography can lead us to a better place. Contemplation allows us to see through God's eyes, as it were, and, in the process, all of creation becomes more wondrous and beautiful. As we pay greater attention, the ordinary becomes extra-ordinary

Photographic contemplation does not just involve the process of slowing down and patiently allowing our camera to receive an image through the release of a shutter or tap of the screen. We can also pause and focus our gaze on photos we have already created or photos other people have made. This can be exciting, as it can reveal things we were not immediately aware of when making a photo or also help us see the world from other people's perspectives. What I see in a picture may be completely different to what you see and, in a world which is fragmented and divided, photography then has the potential to be a powerful tool for greater social cohesion – it helps me to see your world and you to see mine. This can lead to mutual understanding, which can lead to loving respect. Fear often arises when I cannot see or understand your world and you cannot see mine.

As we have shaped this book, we have spent some time considering the difference between Christian contemplation and the increasingly popular practice of mindfulness. We are confident there is a distinction between the two, but the more we have wrestled together trying to differentiate them, the greater we have found the blurring of any boundaries.

A different view of the self distinguishes Christian spirituality from secular mindfulness. Christian contemplation has as its focus a belief that the Holy Spirit will guide our thoughts and emotions and through this our actions. This guidance functions by stilling our minds and helping us notice both what is in front of us and what is within us in the present moment. Secular mindfulness is premised on a similar practice but does not subscribe to the idea that the Holy Spirit guides our actions. Rather, by noticing our emotions and experience in a compassionate moment-by-moment way, our actions to self and others are guided by the enhanced awareness brought by living in the present moment. Christian contemplation is also different insofar as it involves openness to the presence of God directly experienced in one's soul and even, potentially, union with God; as well as devotion to God and the cultivation of self-transcendence and sacrificial love.

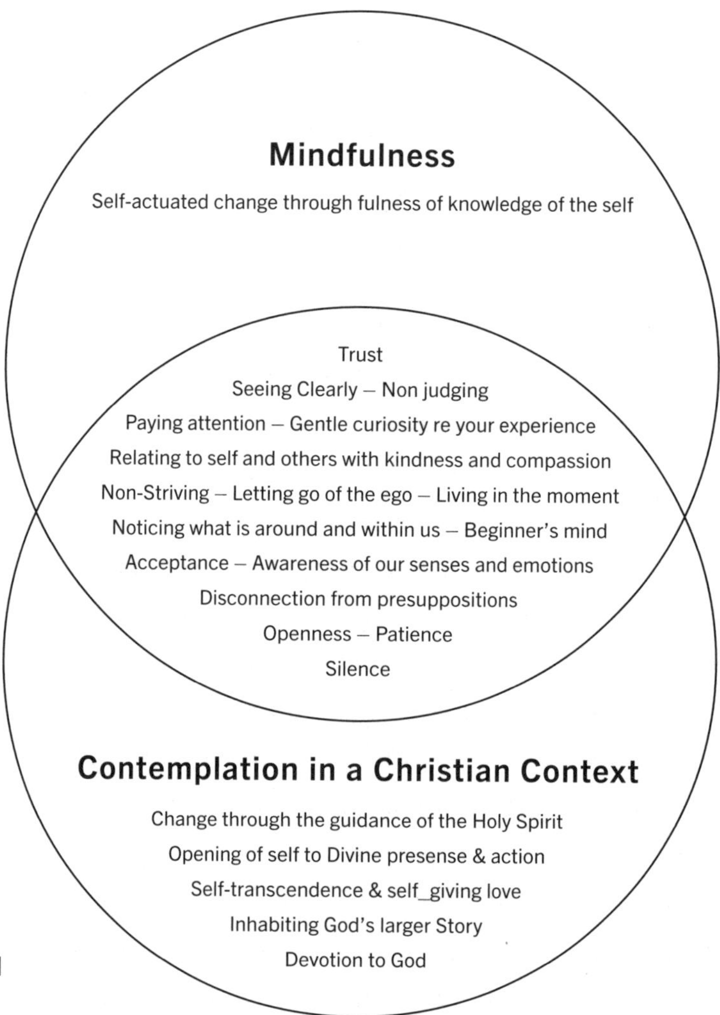

Venn Diagram.
Mindfulness and
Contemplation

We believe it is important to recognise this distinction, but we also believe that mindfulness and the Christian contemplative tradition are closely related and have a broadly similar aim, which is to live life in a fulfilled and compassionate way. One of the early pioneers of mindfulness, Professor Mark Williams, encourages Christians to see God at work in mindfulness. He refers to the biblical prophet Isaiah, who told his exiled compatriots that their freedom would, astonishingly, be accomplished not through a Jewish king but via Cyrus, a Persian king – someone outside their tradition doing the work of God. If Christians insist all they need is to be found within their own tradition, Williams claims, they may well miss out on something which is of God – inspired from outside their tradition and for which they are hungering.[6]

A full investigation into the similarities and differences of mindfulness and Christian contemplation is outside the scope of this book but we wanted to acknowledge the debate and share with you our own struggles in seeking to understand these two traditions. We will use the terms contemplation and mindfulness interchangeably within this book but if you want to explore in more detail the connections between secular mindfulness and Christian contemplation we recommend Tim Stead's book, *Mindfulness and Christian Spirituality* [7] and also Peter Tyler's book, *Christian Mindfulness: Theology and Practice.* [8]

Today we hear a lot about mindfulness and its benefits for our health and wellbeing. It is taught in places as diverse as the school classroom and corporate executive training. It has a vast field of research behind it, pointing to the many benefits of this practice for both our physical and mental wellbeing. Our use of the word 'practice' is significant. In the foreword to Mark Williams and Danny Penman's book, *Mindfulness: a practical guide to finding peace in a frantic world,* Professor Jon Kabat-Zinn draws attention to their understanding of mindfulness which they see as a practice, a way of being, it is not simply a technique or passing fad.[9] The concept comes from a Pali word, 'sati', which is generally translated as mindfulness or awareness and is an important part of Buddhist meditation. At the heart of mindfulness is our ability to 'live in the present moment'.

If you find the idea of living in the present moment too abstract, you might like to understand it as becoming more aware of your emotions and surroundings.

This might sound a bit odd, as we are normally conscious of the place where we are standing or sitting; but to be aware of our emotions and surroundings means more than that. It means noticing how you are feeling (e.g., happy or sad), your bodily sensations (e.g., the feel of the wind on our face) and all the physical details of where you are (e.g., the weather, the sounds, the people, the colours). However, this awareness must be done in a non-judgemental way. In other words, you should not wish you felt differently or found yourself in a different place. It is simply noticing your experience of the present. By encouraging an attitude of acceptance and non-judgement, mindfulness seeks to realise a moment-by-moment awareness of your thoughts, bodily feelings, and environment. As Tim Stead puts it, mindfulness is 'being more fully aware of your own experience in the present moment in a non-judgemental way'.[10]

Being aware of our surroundings and emotions is an important life skill but one we can fail to employ in our daily living because of our tendency to rush through life. It is easy to just think about the next task or appointment, the next promotion or job, perhaps even simply the next meal break or holiday. When this becomes our norm, we miss the beauty that is contained in the present moment. Life literally passes us by because we can never inhabit the future, only the present.

The marriage of the smartphone with the camera means many of us have a camera available to us all the time. In this book we aim to introduce how photography can be a mindful activity and provide some practical examples. We believe the accessibility and popularity of photography through the smartphone provides an easy way into mindfulness. Rather than learning something completely new, mindful photography seeks to adapt what we are already doing to bring the benefits of mindfulness into our everyday life. We are not suggesting this book is a replacement for the excellent courses on mindfulness that are available, but rather a companion to them. Since this book is not purely a book about mindfulness you will of course learn more about the breadth and practices of mindfulness on specific courses.[11] However, we recognise not everyone has the time or the resources to access such a course. We hope this book will at least be a helpful small step into mindfulness and be a benefit to those who have tried mindfulness courses but struggle with its practice on a daily basis.

The first step of mindful photography is our ability to be aware of the present moment, noticing the things we see around us and how our bodies feel, the climate and how the cold wind or warm sunshine feels on our skin, how we are feeling emotionally, the noises that surround us, the colours and textures of the things we see, and suchlike. In mindful photography we don't pick up a camera in the hope of photographing a specific picture, in fact we should never venture out with a camera in hand with a picture in mind. This is what differentiates mindful photography from other photographic genres. For example, a wedding photographer starts their day with a set of images they know they must achieve before the day has finished (for instance, bridal, groom and couple portraits, group pictures, the first kiss, the first dance, etc.). A landscape photographer will climb a hillside early in the morning to photograph a particular landscape bathed with the golden hour's light. A wildlife photographer might have a particular animal or behaviour they hope to see and photograph.

Within mindful photography we leave our camera in its bag or our pocket until we feel a connection with wherever we are. That connection arises by noticing and becoming aware of our physical surroundings and our emotions, and, once that happens, the wonder of the present opens before us. Mindful photography is open to mystery and surprise, never knowing what each moment will hold. It is a genre of photography which is free from judgement — the idea that a picture can be good or bad — and filled with wonder and revelation. We never 'take' pictures, but rather receive them as a gift, recognising our place as co-creators with the picture we are receiving. There is no conquest in contemplative photography — the picture is not about how many likes we get on social media or our desire to win a competition with it — but rather a recognition of our interconnectedness with everything in the present moment.

The photographer Ruth Davey describes mindful photography as 'a tool that uses our sight and the lens of our camera or smartphone as an anchor to help us become more consciously aware of and connected to the present moment. It is experiencing the process of creating photographs in a non-judgemental way, with gratitude and compassion towards ourselves, others and the world around us. It enables us to slow down, look again and see our lives differently.'[12]

Wellbeing

Mindfulness is often seen as an aid to wellbeing. New businesses are springing up on what seems a daily basis, offering retreats and workshops designed to improve our wellbeing.

A quick search we undertook on the photography social media platform Instagram™ found the hashtag #wellbeing revealed just under 12 million images and #health revealed just under 150 million images, whilst #healing revealed just under 33 million images.

What is fascinating about these hashtags is how many of the images show something outside a formal healthcare setting. Many of the images reflect an interconnectedness with nature and other people, such as pictures of massage, holding hands, breaking free, sunsets or beaches.

We believe that by making small adaptations to the way we use our camera, allowing us to receive images mindfully, our wellbeing has the potential to be strengthened. The marriage of the smartphone and the camera gives us a unique opportunity to strengthen our personal resilience and, as we'll see, it could also open to us ancient avenues of wellbeing, long forgotten by modern society, called, *visio divina* and the Book of Hours. Some people find the term wellbeing unhelpful. If this is true for you, try using the words 'flourishing' or 'thriving' instead, as in many ways this is what wellbeing is actually describing.

The New Economics Foundation defines wellbeing as 'how people feel and how they function, both on a personal and a social level, and how they evaluate their lives as a whole.'[13] It is more than the absence of disease and has as its focus how we feel about life and how we function within life. The term 'being' within the word, wellbeing, is important as it reminds us that our identity is derived from more than what we do. There is a danger in Western living that we define ourselves through our work. When introduced to a new person our first question is often, 'what do you do?' This can be a difficult question to answer if we do not have a job or are unhappy in our work and can harm our sense of worth. When we define ourselves through what we do, we become human-doings, not human-beings.

Our 'being' encompasses our environment, our bodies, the things we do and enjoy, the people who share our lives in different ways, and our communities, as well as our beliefs and spirituality, how we make sense of life and what it means to be alive and engaged. There can be no single way in which to measure our wellbeing as we are all different. However, medical professionals have devised a model to help understand our wellbeing called the 'Warwick-Edinburgh-Mental-Well-Being Scale (WEMWBS).[14] The scale includes positively worded questions to help understand a person's mental health in terms of both how they are feeling and how they are functioning. As we will explore later in this book, feelings and emotions are an important and often overlooked dimension of being human. We sometimes downplay feelings when we criticise others, saying, for instance, 'don't be so emotional!' Emotions are a form of knowledge that can often tell us something quite important about ourselves. As we will see, the practice of *visio divina* in particular places a strong emphasis on the world of feelings.

Research undertaken by The New Economics Foundation for the UK Government sought to identify behaviours which can benefit our wellbeing.[15] They identified five behaviours which characterise people who have good mental wellbeing. They are simply called 'The Five Steps to Wellbeing'. These steps are promoted by the NHS and mental health charities such as the UK's Mind charity. An exciting thing about looking at these behaviours in relation to photography is how easily they can be integrated into the process of taking pictures. We will outline these steps briefly below with a short explanation of how they can be integrated into photography.

1. **Connect**. Evidence suggests that feeling close to and valued by others is an important human need. Photography allows us to connect with other people in many ways. It might be by posting an image on social media or other ways

we share pictures together of our lives — for example, the times we get our phones out and say, 'Let me show you my holiday ...'. It can also be good fun to intentionally go out together with someone else to take some pictures. But connection involves more than other people. We will suggest in this book that photography can help us realise our interconnectedness with all of nature. When we photograph a bee collecting pollen on a flower, we see not only the beauty of the flower that we have perhaps tended in our garden and an insect collecting its lunch, we also see a vital part of our ecosystem and our own food chain. When we photograph a tree, we can also recognise that stood there is a symbiotic relationship with our lungs, as it were — what *we* breathe out sustains the tree and what *it* breathes out, sustains us.

2. **Be Active**. Exercise is linked to good mental health. Photography can help encourage us to be active within our own limits. We can let our camera take us for a walk, as it were, and connect with our environment. If we cannot get out of our house, we can be active within it; it is amazing what there is to see right under our noses when we pause to really look.

3. **Take Notice**. We rush through life, maybe getting children ready for school, running for the bus, working through the pile of paper on our desk, and we often do not have time to notice the beauty around us. Research has shown that when we 'take time' to notice what is happening around us our wellbeing is enhanced and our life priorities can be reaffirmed. We think we need lots of time to 'take notice', but within this book we will explore some basic photography skills which can help us slow down and become more attentive. You will find it only takes a moment to 'take notice' and this can be incorporated into your daily activities. Mindfulness does not have to involve sitting cross-legged for an hour or more trying to focus on our breathing! A moment's pause is all you need. Using our cameras or looking at photos can be a great way to facilitate such pauses which enable us to 'take notice'.

4. **Learn.** Learning can enhance our self-esteem and encourage us to be more mentally active. Within this book we hope you will learn something about the techniques of mindful photography. Through this we hope you will learn to see yourself, one another, the divine, and nature in new ways which show our interconnectedness.

5. **Give.** According to the mental health charity, Mind, individuals who report a greater interest in helping others are more likely to rate themselves as happy. An important part of photography is sharing our images with other people. Images can reveal lots about us, including our hopes, dreams and fears. Through this process we reveal something of our self and learn about one another. The gifts we can bring are acceptance and attentive ears, as people share their images, which can help us all thrive. For some of us it can be hard to share our pictures as we fear being judged, but we hope everyone has at least one person with whom they can risk sharing a picture. Having the courage to take this step can lead to many wonderful conversations and help deepen our relationships.

In our lives we are on a journey together and we have so much we can learn from one another. We hope this book might contribute to that learning in some small way, but more importantly we hope it will provide a spark for your own learning and engagement with life, opening new directions and understanding. Our hope is that this book would help you and those closest to you to see yourself and the world with compassion and love as you receive the gift of mindful and contemplative photography.

Photography and wellbeing – personal accounts

From war to wonder – Steve Radley

Photography has been a part of Steve's life from the time his dad introduced him to his darkroom (a room which was dark except a dim red light where films used to be developed). To a young boy it was a magical place as you literally saw pictures appear on the photographic paper as it sat in the developer chemicals.

As a youngster Steve suffered at times from what would be called anxiety today, but he discovered taking his camera out helped calm any anxious thinking. As film was expensive, he would sometimes take pictures without any film in the camera – just go through the process of slowing down, framing and pressing the shutter.

After school, Steve worked on farms for a short time, giving him a love of nature, before moving to agricultural college, where his studies included business management which led to a career in business. Then, in the mid-1990s, Steve felt called to ordination in the Church, and so trained and was ordained as a priest in the Church of England.

Much of Steve's ordained ministry has centred on the military as an RAF chaplain, seeing him travel around the world to some very challenging places including the Gulf and Afghanistan. These experiences of war, which exposed him to a lot of suffering and death, left him suffering from anxiety and flashbacks – finding it difficult to mix in large crowds.

Steve received medical help for these experiences, but he also started to study for a diploma in photography. He found the photography had a calming effect on his mind and emotions, the camera became a tool for mindfulness and contemplation without realising it. As Steve learnt more about waiting, noticing, seeing light, composition, texture, story and all the things associated with photography, he found some of his anxieties became easier to manage and flashbacks became less prevalent in his life. The camera literally helped him slow down and engage in life in new ways.

Many people who survive trauma find positive change as well as the flashbacks and survivor guilt they may experience. It can manifest itself in, for example, a new appreciation for life, a newfound personal strength or focus on helping others; and this was something Steve found happened with the help of his photography. He suddenly saw the incredible beauty in ordinary things like clouds blowing across the sky, the intricate nature of flowers, the purposefulness of a bee collecting nectar and he now always pauses to look at these things. The busyness of life can mean we miss the beauty of the ordinary, because the ordinary becomes so familiar.

Steve's experience can be described through a theory called post traumatic growth where people realise a new appreciation of life. For Steve this growth happened with the help of his camera, which helps him slow down, focus on the present moment, and notice the wonder of the world we are blessed to inhabit.

You can learn more about Steve's work at: www.soulfulvision.uk

From Fleet Street to landscape – Paul Sanders

Paul Sanders always had a need to prove himself, to push his limits, to succeed. That desire led to a high-flying career in newspaper photography. The only place he ever wanted to work was for a national newspaper. Pushing himself to the absolute limits to attain his goals, Paul sacrificed everything for it, including friendships and relationships, and became incredibly selfish throughout this journey.

By 2002, he was working for *The Times* newspaper and by 2004, was Picture Editor, reviewing nearly 20,000 images each day, running a team of about 33 people with a huge budget and being responsible for all the visual content of the newspaper. The success he'd sought in his early career as a photographer was right in front of him. However, as much as he enjoyed the job, he began to feel that something was missing. The time that Paul spent at home became shorter and shorter. The time he had to himself was diminished and gradually his life became mere existence. At the same time, his marriage was falling apart and his relationship with his son had become non-existent.

As a result of these pressures, Paul found himself in a bad way. He suffered with severe depression, insomnia, an eating disorder, and had self-harmed. He began to feel utterly worthless. Towards the end of 2011, he suffered from a nervous breakdown and at his lowest point went down to the clifftop at Beachy Head with the thought of ending his life.

He had absolutely no sense of what he was doing, who he was, where he was. Paul simply knew that he didn't want to exist anymore. Strangely, at that point, feeling lost and alone, he said a prayer and, as Paul sat there contemplating if and when he would actually jump, a man came to talk to him. He sat with Paul and just talked to him about why he was there. The man listened and spoke without judgement and, by the time he had finished, Paul found himself in tears, knowing that suicide would be no way out for him.

As they walked away from the edge of that cliff, Paul felt a tremendous weight lift and a warmth surround him, almost like a hug. It made him realise that he was being truly looked after, truly saved, and being given another chance. He took to praying a lot after that and listening for the responses. Rather than asking for things, he just asked for help.

Through his reflection and prayer, Paul realised he needed to simplify his life. He needed to strip away all the things that were unnecessary, all the things he'd sought for in his career: the success, money, and kudos. He left *The Times* at the end of 2011 and started as a freelance landscape photographer, with no prior experience of landscape photography at all. He really did not know what he was doing or where to begin. He just knew that this was a direction that was helping.

Landscape photography became his therapy. It allows Paul to have a greater connection with the world around him, to be completely present in what he's doing, and, importantly, allows time with God. His photography also helped him open up in therapy about his mental health problems. Using his photographs as a vehicle for conversation with his therapist was easier than just speaking.

Paul can sit while he's taking photographs and pray. As he sees the incredible created beauty around him, he feels a deep connection with God. Somehow, through the landscape in front of him mediated by his camera, he feels God really speaks to him. The connection with God is stronger when he's outside and he says he can feel that God is, as it were, 'sitting right next to me, almost like we're having a chat'.

Today, Paul uses his photography to help others and gives talks to support people, especially those with mental illness and depression. He finds that through photography he's able to freely discuss these issues. He talks openly about his own issues and the journey that he's been on; he says that, if others feel a connection to God through that, then that's good and may help initiate their own faith journey.

You can learn more about Paul's work at: www.discoverstill.com

CHAPTER 2

Exploring meanings in photos – from theological reflection to *visio divina*

Illustrative approach

Once a photo has been taken it can become something that we and others glance at and dismiss or, instead, something that captures our attention or curiosity and makes us pause to look in more detail and reflect on what we're seeing. Photos can become things that we linger with and ponder, as we explore their meaning. They may be our own photos or those that others have taken. The image that we record will initially reflect our own take on a scene, a person or a situation, but once created it will have a life of its own. Other viewers may find different meanings in the photo than the ones we intended and we may see things in our own images that we hadn't originally noticed. For instance, when Philip was photographing a Sunday market in Italy it wasn't until he reviewed the photos afterwards that he noticed this image of a teenager imploring someone, probably her mother, to let her buy something – her eyes are closed and her hands are folded, as if in prayer. It was this photo that became emblematic for the 'Sunday' photo essay that he was creating. But he hadn't noticed the girl's actions at the time.

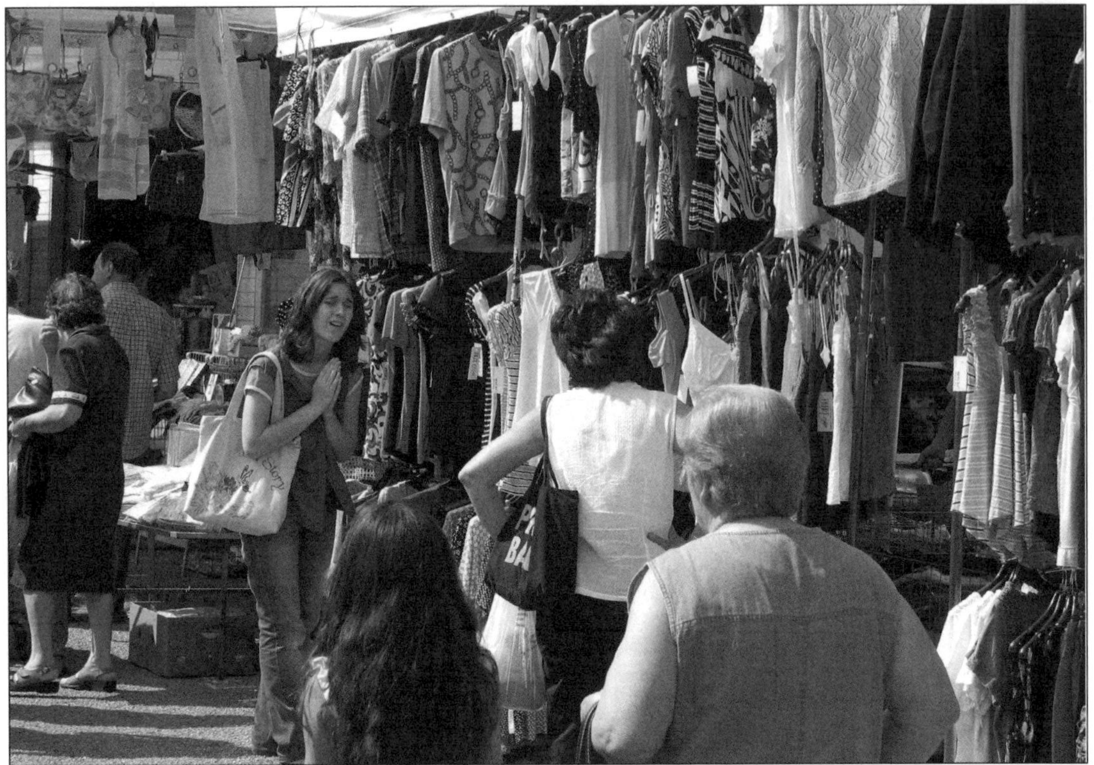

Italian Sunday Market © Philip Richter

Sometimes you may consciously be taking photos that you hope might become images for people (including yourself) to meditate on. For example, you may choose to take a set of images to illustrate a verse from the Bible or a prayer or a hymn. Imagine, for instance, how you might illustrate Fred Kaan's hymn, 'Put peace into each other's hands',[16] with its strongly visual symbolism. Kevin Hooke's photo book, *A Dartmoor Psalter: reflecting on the Psalms using images of Dartmoor* (Blurb, 2016), offers a set of personal reflections on the Psalms through his photography. His evocative pictures of Dartmoor well illustrate and complement his written reflections. The photos help you to meditate on, and pause within, the words of the psalms. They also potentially help you hold the words in your memory. What Kevin doesn't do, but could have done, is to engage in an extended exploration of and meditation on the photos themselves in their own right, rather than simply using them to illustrate his writing. Though once or twice he begins to do that, for instance, when he meditates on Psalm 65:

'I was busying myself taking pictures and didn't see the rain coming in until it started. I was only about a mile from the car, but having come out without anything waterproof (when will I learn?!) a mile was far enough, and I was pleased to get into the dry. Inwardly I grumbled about the weather, my luck and my stupidity! It is not always easy to get satisfying photographs of the moor in rain – everything just turned grey and misty – and cameras and water don't mix very well, so I settled for this shot of a dripping gate catch. What I hadn't previously appreciated is that there are several places in the psalms where rainfall is especially described as God's blessing – a gift and a sign of his care.'[17]

Meditating subsequently on the photo he had hurriedly taken, Kevin was able to appreciate new depths of meaning in Psalm 65.

Discovery approach

If we describe the general approach of *A Dartmoor Psalter* as the 'illustrative' way to creating reflective photos, there is also an alternative 'discovery' approach to reflective photography. The 'discovery' approach relies on you finding an image, either one that someone else has already taken or an image that you notice and yourself photograph. The idea is that you don't go out with a preconceived idea of the image you want to find: you simply find an image that draws your attention. The great twentieth-century spiritual writer, Thomas Merton, advised photographers to: 'Stop looking and ... begin seeing! Because looking means that you already have something in mind for your eye to find; you've set out in search of your desired object and have closed off everything else presenting itself along the way. But seeing is being open and receptive to what comes to the eye.'[18]

Once you have a photo you want to reflect on you may choose to do this mostly with your mind (this can be called 'reflecting theologically') or mostly with your heart (this can be what is called '*visio divina*'), though both can cross over into the other. The first approach, which focuses more on your mind, reflects on the photo in the light of Scripture, our Christian heritage, and our own and others' experience of God. An example of this is David Perry's 'Thinking big' reflection in *The Connexion* magazine (7, Winter/Spring 2017).[19] Here, David Perry reflects on his own photo of the London Shard juxtaposed with a weather-worn wooden cross, taken from the precinct of Southwark Cathedral. 'The cross', he says, 'invites us to see our surroundings differently by setting the scene from God's outlook, not ours. In this respect the Shard is comically diminutive, for as a standpoint from which to gain a breathtakingly awesome view it is hopelessly outclassed and outperformed by the humble wooden cross … Why? Because it is from the cross, and the lofty vantage point of Christ's risen presence alone, that we can believe and know in the heart of our being that there is nothing love cannot face.' So, this photo takes on special meaning as the photographer reflects on the meaning of the cross in Christian belief and experience. Further reflections on photos by David Perry can be found in his 'visualtheology' blog.[20]

We will return to another example of David Perry's photographic theological reflection shortly. In the meantime, what do we mean by theological reflection and how might photos have an even more prominent place within it?

The term 'theological reflection' might sound a little daunting, as if it can only be done by trained practitioners. In fact, theological reflection is simply to do with making active connections between everyday life and faith. It's about focusing on significant life events or dilemmas and holding them up to the light of Christian tradition, seen through theology, Church history or Scripture. And, vice versa, it's to do with reappraising Christian tradition through the lens of everyday experience. At its best, theological reflection enables more faithful and authentic Christian discipleship.

'Reflection' is, of course, a word that applies in English both to thought and to light. Both senses of the word derive from the Latin verb, 'reflectere', meaning 'to bend back'. A reflective surface literally bends back light rays to the eye, whilst in reflective thinking your thoughts are turned back, as it were, to reconsider past experiences, actions and ideas. Reflection happens in both senses when you use a printed photo to aid reflection — unlike an image on an electronic screen, a print does not emit light and merely reflects.

Gary O'Neill has described how students training for licensed and ordained ministry in the Church of England through the 'All Saints Centre for Mission and Ministry', were artfully introduced to principles and practice of theological reflection without the term being initially used. At the time, Gary was Director of Studies at All Saints. He described a forty-five minute activity that new students would undertake on their induction day. It took place in a small hall and began with a slide show of photos of homeless people living on the streets of Manchester.

After viewing the photos, students were invited to write responses to what they had seen on post-it notes in the four corners of the room. Each corner had a different focus. In one corner they were asked what they thought Scripture says about homelessness. In another corner they were asked to speculate on how the world they lived in regarded homelessness — how, for instance, would different newspapers headline their reports about homeless people? In another corner the students were invited to share any personal experiences of homelessness or interacting with homeless people. In the final corner they were asked about their own instinctive or emotive reactions to homelessness.

The students were then invited to revisit each corner and have conversations with others about their responses, if they wished. Finally, they were encouraged to mingle in the middle of the hall and share their experiences of the activity they had just completed. It was only at this point that it was revealed to students that they had received a 'slightly under the radar' introduction to theological reflection and to the particular model favoured at All Saints — a 'four source' approach drawing on Tradition, Culture, Experience and Position, as represented by the activities in the four corners of the hall.[21]

The model of theological reflection used at All Saints was one of many possible approaches. It will have been important for the students later to have had finely focused engagement with the model, to have applied proper self-criticism and to have displayed openness to the presence and activity of God. One interesting thing, however, is that this model directly engages with images, albeit normally participants' own drawings. There is, arguably, good scope for potentially using photos on a regular basis within this model.

The model was originally developed by John de Beer for the global 'Education for Ministry' (EfM) lay development course, based at the Sewanee University of the South School of Theology in Tennessee. It presupposes four sources of wisdom or meaning in people's lives: Personal Experience, Faith Tradition, Contemporary Culture, and Personal Belief/Position,[22] on which participants draw to theologically reflect on a particular incident, problem, belief, item from Christian tradition or cultural aspect. The process begins by carefully identifying a critical focus for the reflection: the heart of the matter. The next step is to translate that into an image. For instance, if you chose to focus on the biblical text Genesis 1:31 ('God saw everything that he had made, and indeed, it was very good') you might decide to create an image that expresses what it would be like to experience 'life as very good': for instance, 'an ordinary box that contains a wonderful gift'.[23] From now on the image takes centre-stage, rather than the original focus. The image bridges between the four sources and makes for a creative conversation between them. The model can be graphically represented as a tetrahedron with the image at its centre. Use of an image promotes a more spacious, less prescriptive style of theological reflection and 'deliberately encourages the evocative, intuitive quality of exploration'.[24] As such, it helps prevent theological reflection from becoming too cerebral and conceptual and, instead, arguably gives proper scope for emotion and imagination.

Next comes 'exploring' which involves asking some theological questions of the focusing image: such as, when life is like the image, what can bring 'wholeness, brokenness, recognition, reorientation, and restoration?'[25] Exploring then segues into connecting: discovering links with and between the four sources. For example, the image we have already mentioned might bring to mind depictions of a very good life from contemporary culture and this might be compared and contrasted with perspectives on the good life drawn from Christian tradition. Finally, the model moves into applying and working out the implications of this theological reflection for one's beliefs, attitudes, values and actions.

As we have seen, this approach to theological reflection puts an image, such as a photo or drawing, centre-stage. However, unlike David Perry's reflection on the Cross and Shard (see above), the starting point is not the image but rather a presenting issue, incident or puzzle. The image then plays a pivotal role in the resulting theological reflection.

We can use the EfM model as a framework for seeing how David Perry engaged in theological reflection in a post on his Visualtheology blog, entitled 'COP out 26: valuing our precious planet'.[26] This is not to imply that he himself explicitly applied the EfM model in the blog, but it demonstrates how he echoes aspects of the EfM approach and, in this case, places his photo centre-stage. The starting point for his piece is a life event which throws up disconcerting issues for planet earth – he is writing just after the end of the UN Climate Change Conference (COP26) held in Glasgow in the autumn of 2021. As the title to his piece indicates, David fears that COP26 was a 'cop out': there had been a failure to properly address the pressing issues of human-induced climate change and it was a case of 'all too little and too late'.

He identifies one of his photos from his back catalogue, taken at some point before COP26, which seems to encapsulate his sense of frustration. The photo is of the multi-toned, ochre-coloured globe centrepiece of the Swirle Pavillion in Newcastle upon Tyne. Already, when he first made the image, he had been struck by how it resembled a globe on fire and it had brought to mind the earth's vulnerability to global heating because of the climate crisis. Now, after COP26, he notices the steel latticework surrounding the globe, which seems to David like a cage imprisoning the globe. The image speaks to him of negative aspects of contemporary culture: the 'mantra of prosperity and profit' driving developed economies and the vested interests of those profiting from fossil fuels, impeding change. In other words, it becomes an image that represents corporate sin.

His theological reflection then effectively brings the three other sources of wisdom identified by the EfM model into conversation. He draws on his personal experience of extreme weather events in the UK attributable to climate change and confesses that the outlook for the future of the planet seems 'terrifying' and that it will be 'such a daunting task' to successfully tackle climate change. He draws on his personal belief and positions, asserting his fundamental conviction that 'the earth is the Lord's and all that is within it' (Psalm 24:1) and embracing his own lifestyle choices, such as investing in an electric car, switching to a mostly plant-based diet and committing to green energy and green politics. David also compares and contrasts contemporary culture's attitude to the climate emergency with that of his faith tradition. Drawing on Judaeo-Christian Tradition, he receives a strong sense of 'the inherent worth of all life' and of the necessity of looking after the whole cosmos as a gift from God. He grounds this in the creation poetry of Genesis, the inspired holistic visions of Isaiah and Psalm 24. Alongside the negative aspects of contemporary culture, he also discovers other more positive strands that chime with this biblical vision, such as a green agenda: 'a vision of true prosperity, measured not in terms of money or GDP but of the wellbeing and flourishing of all life'.

Meanwhile, David's perception of the globe photo has subtly changed. It began with a sense of the globe representing a planet on fire; it later seemed that the globe was imprisoned within a latticework cage; ultimately, he begins to see the steel latticework in much more positive and wholesome terms, as representing 'a set of values and sustainable practices which seek to protect the earth and keep its peoples from harm'. The image of the globe has, as it were, turned full circle as David's reflections have encompassed different sources of wisdom, looking for the truth in each and allowing them to speak to each other. The photographic image has remained centre-stage throughout, helping to mediate that encounter, and, in the process, is eventually itself seen in a new light and as a spur to releasing faithful action and discipleship. The photo that once spoke of sin now speaks of potential redemption. And so, the reflection ends on a more positive note with a call to adopt 'green strategies in our own daily lives' and to lobby for change.

As we have seen here, it's possible for photo and text to complement each other on equal terms. The photo is not simply used to illustrate what is said in the accompanying text. Neither does the text merely amount to an extensive caption for the photo. It is, potentially, a symbiotic relationship, powerfully integrating photo and text.

Visio divina

We move now from considering reflective approaches to letting photos speak, primarily involving one's mind, to another method, rooted in Christian spirituality and focusing particularly on the heart – *visio divina*. We'll be exploring some of the history and practice of *visio divina*, as it relates to artistic creations and, more specifically, your own or others' photos. *Visio divina* is a Latin term which translates as 'divine seeing' or 'sacred seeing'.

But first let's take a glance at its near neighbour, *lectio divina* – 'divine' or 'sacred' reading. *Lectio divina* is the unhurried, patient, prayerful and transformative reading of Scripture, as practised down the centuries by monks and nuns and more recently revived as a contemporary spiritual practice. Both *lectio divina* and *visio divina* could be seen as resonating with the so-called 'Slow Movement', which began in Italy in the 1980s as a reaction against the prioritising of speed over quality of life in modern culture. Consumption of and exposure to written text or visual media is deliberately slowed down so that you have the opportunity to listen with the *ears* of the heart, in the case of *lectio divina*, and see with the *eyes* of the heart, in the case of *visio divina*.

Lectio divina is quite different from the skim-reading that is prevalent in today's society and its plundering of texts for easily digested information. It is a form of religious reading intended to bring a person closer to God and, as it were, to 'read God' and take God's Word to heart. *Lectio divina* is a form of slow reading, in which the reader lingers on the words, savours and ponders them, much like reading poetry or a much-treasured love letter. Readers may choose to quietly read the text out aloud or memorise content, reinforcing the sense that the words are addressed to them and God's love is personally for them. The adjective 'divina' refers not only to the reading matter, the 'Word of God', but also to the style of reading: at its best, it is 'reading done … with God, a heart-to-heart … even more, it is reading that bears a love message for me from the God who seeks me'.[27]

Traditionally, *lectio divina* has been seen in terms of four stages or four 'rungs on a ladder', as Prior Guigo II famously summarised it back in the twelfth century. It begins with reading, and then moves through meditation, prayer and contemplation. The first rung, reading, involves calm careful attention to the text, reading the passage several times, 'gently listening to hear a word or phrase that is God's word for us this day'. The second rung, meditation, involves unhurried mulling over the passage, patiently pondering it and allowing it to 'interact with our thoughts, our hopes, our memories, our desires'. The third rung, prayer, involves dialogue with God and allowing God's Word 'to touch and change our deepest selves'. The final rung, contemplation, takes the reader beyond the text and invites them wordlessly to rest in God's presence, 'simply enjoying the experience of being in the presence of God.'[28] In short, 'reading seeks for the sweetness of a blessed life, meditation perceives it, prayer asks for it, contemplation tastes it.'[29]

Historically, *visio divina* and *lectio divina* are close cousins and there is an evident overlap between the two as we seek to 'read' as well as 'see' pictures. The focus on seeing in *visio divina* encompasses our emotional responses to images as well as our intellectual processing of what we see. It concerns the heart, traditionally thought of as the seat of our emotions and feelings. Pictures strike an emotional chord within us which is why they are used so prevalently in advertising and the media. When we see a picture of a child suffering on a newspaper front page, our first response is often to feel upset or angry that such injustice exists in the world. This feeling precedes our reading of the article printed below the picture which will give us context and usually the opinion of the journalist who wrote the article. We may later analyse what we have seen with our mind to better understand why the situation exists and we may also use our mind to formulate a personal response to what we have seen — for instance, perhaps we will choose to donate to a charity which helps reduce the suffering we have seen and provoked our initial emotional response of anger or sadness. This example reflects the intertwining of our emotional response (the heart) and our thinking (the mind). Within Christianity we can see the mutual importance given to both heart and mind through the command of Jesus to '*Love the Lord your God with all your heart and with all your soul and with all your mind.*'[30] The heart is usually considered to be the seat of our emotions and the Christian Scriptures support this idea; for example, Jesus promises that his followers' hearts will rejoice.[31] When addressing some religious leaders, Jesus asks why they are thinking evil things in their hearts.[32] Here Jesus clearly connects feelings and emotions to thought processes, as we may have done just now when considering the newspaper picture that depicted suffering.

Within Western culture, we tend towards an emphasis on knowledge gained through the thought processes of our mind and see these thoughts as separate to and superior to our emotions. Rational thought, it is believed, belongs in the mind; the emotions can lead us down an alley of false knowledge. This emphasis in the West on the mind means there can be a danger that we see our bodies as merely a means to house our brains; but, as the words of Jesus we cited above suggest, our emotions and our minds are related – one cannot exist without the other, and neither exist without the body. We sometimes talk about a 'gut feeling' or 'butterflies in our stomach' which reflects how much our bodies are involved. The linking of heart and mind and body in Scripture reminds us that our emotional knowledge is important, and both our emotions and rational thoughts are of crucial importance in our learning and understanding of ourselves and the world around us. In the world of psychology there is an increasing interest and research in terms of the interlinking of our minds, body and emotions. For instance, the psychiatrist, Bessel van der Kolk, argues that we cannot ignore the place of the body in our understanding of trauma which his research suggests reshapes both the body and the brain.[33] In a similar way when we hold our rational thought, bodily response and emotional response in tandem when reflecting on an event our whole being can be reshaped. Within the Christian tradition this has been seen in terms of the potential to become more Christlike – where our bodies, feelings and minds are reshaped to reflect the image of the perfect human believed to be seen in the person of Jesus Christ.

Religions have long understood the importance of body, heart and mind and have used the arts and creativity as a means for encountering the divine and drawing these three aspects of our being together. Buildings used as places of worship perhaps offer the most common and visible form of the use of the arts in worship and divine encounter. Think of the symmetry and pattern found in English cathedrals, or the colour and vibrance found in an Indian Buddhist temple. Such examples show how, historically, religions have used art as a place to draw us into an encounter with the divine through our emotional response and our embodiment of that response.

It is worth noting that art has also been used as a means of teaching religious truth, for example, stained glass is not always simply decorative. It is also a medium through which the central messages of the Christian faith are expressed. This is most obvious with the stained glass from the medieval and Renaissance periods. Literacy was not as widespread in those days and the church used stained glass and other artworks to teach the central tenets of the Christian faith.

In his book, *Pictures and Tears*, the artist, James Elkins, is fascinated by the ability of art to move us, as the title suggests, to tears.[34] He notes that some pictures which create this emotional response are not necessarily depicting a sad scene, but still touch something deep within our psyche. Elkin found that the type of art which created this response was varied, including representational art, abstract art, and pieces from different periods. Art in its many forms seems to connect with something deep within us.

Elkins cannot provide a reason for why this might be, but still finds it intriguing. The art historian, Rachel Smith, addressing the Calvin Symposium on worship suggests a Christian worldview can help explain the response noted by Elkins. Smith suggests art allows us to see something longed for, but equally that which we cannot yet fully experience or have immediately.[35] Hope, for example, is by definition oriented towards the future and something we are unable to fully claim ownership of in this present world. Viewed in this way, art allows us a glimpse beyond our present reality, to glimpse something as the divine sees it, and glimpse something of the divine within and around us.

Visio divina is based on the sense of sight, but moves us beyond the physical realms of seeing to grasp a greater reality within all things. In the film, *American Beauty*, the troubled teenager Ricky shows his friend something he has recorded on his camcorder which he describes as the most beautiful thing he has ever filmed. It is simply a discarded carrier bag dancing in the wind. In this scene Ricky was not intentionally practising *visio divina* and he does not have any explicit religious faith, but in his subsequent reflection on what he had seen he appears to have stumbled upon the very heart of this ancient practice. Ricky says, 'Yesterday I realised there was this entire life behind things. And this incredibly benevolent force wanted me to realise there was no reason to be afraid … Sometimes there's so much beauty in the world, I feel that I cannot take it, and my heart is going to cave in.'[36]

Historically, *visio divina* has focused on art or iconography. Within the Eastern Orthodox tradition *visio divina* is practised through icon veneration. There can be a misconception about this practice that the icon is being worshipped, but in fact the icon is simply seen or 'read' as a connecting point between earthly and heavenly realities. The premise of engaging with an icon is that the icon provides a window to heaven and shows something beyond our ordinary physical experience. As the icon is itself a physical object, it reminds the viewer not to reject their physical life but to transform it. Icons are not considered to be painted, but rather drawn, because they are not a creation of the imagination but rather writings of things not of this world which cannot be put into words. Icons are a way in which we are called into a relationship with the family of God which comes before us and extends beyond us for all eternity.

The use of photos for *visio divina* is more recent, which is not surprising given the invention of photography is relatively recent. Photography literally means 'drawing with light' which has echoes of the Orthodox understanding that icons are drawn not created. There is no clear dividing line between *visio divina* with photos, on the one hand, and with art images, on the other hand. Some art images, but not all, are based strongly in an actual place, person or event and are as finely detailed as a photo. Whilst some, but not all, photos, are abstract and others are substantially fabricated. From the earliest days of photography, there has been the opportunity for manipulation of images in the darkroom and, more recently, in post-processing software and, for example, 'magic erasure' capabilities on some smartphones. The application of AI (Artificial Intelligence) has further blurred the difference between artistic creation and photography. For instance, the DALL·E AI online image generator[37] produces a realistic digital image from any descriptive text provided by users. There is an ongoing debate about whether photos heavily indebted to AI should actually be regarded as examples of artistic creativity, rather than photography.

Whilst it is usual to participate with *visio divina* through an icon, painting or a picture, the photographer, Therese Kay, encourages us to remember that any scene or an object can be used as a basis for *visio divina*. Although our book looks at photography and pictures, it is important to remember that if a photograph is not available to us, or we do not have a camera with us when a scene or object makes us stop and pause, we can in that moment practise *visio divina* to help us see deeper into that which has made us pause. The way in which we enter this time is the same rhythm as we describe below when using a photograph, except you are actually looking at the scene or object. Kay has a worked example of using a bone needle on her website which we would recommend reading if you want to extend this practice beyond photography.[38]

As we have already highlighted, there are multiple ways to engage with *visio divina* as a spiritual practice, including using icons or artistic objects, but within this book we are interested in its use through photography. Similarly to *lectio divina*, there is a fourfold movement of looking (rather than reading), meditation, prayer and contemplation. This is the rhythm of using a photo to practise *visio divina* that Steve introduces in his workshops; as you will notice, this rhythm mirrors that of *lectio divina*:

First find a photograph. This can be an old picture or a more recent one. It could be one of your own pictures, a friend's or a picture from a book or magazine. You can engage with this practice on your own, but it can be powerful to do this with another person or group. At the end you can share the different ways in which the photograph has spoken to you.

Reading. Having found your picture, sit comfortably and place it in front of you and close your eyes. Become aware of your breathing, the physical reality which connects us to all of creating. As you breathe in, imagine God's grace and love filling your body and entering your heart at the centre of your being. As you breathe out, imagine that love flowing out into all creation. Allow your breaths to be steady and deep, pulling down from the diaphragm.

Now gently open your eyes and allow them to fall onto your picture with a soft gaze. Do not judge the picture, simply look. As you look allow your eyes to scan the whole picture. Something which can help is to look at the picture as we read a book. Move your eye to the top left corner and scan across to the top right, allow your eyes to drop a little and scan again from left to right. Repeat this until you reach the bottom of the picture.

As you look with a soft gaze, notice the colours, textures, objects, any people, any animals, light and shadows. Allow your eye to be drawn to one area of the picture and allow your gentle gaze to rest on this place.

Meditation. Notice any feelings that arise within you, be aware of any memories that enter your mind or passages from Scripture or other literature. The picture may seem to have no relation to the memory, emotion or passage, but somewhere a connection has been made, so treasure this feeling or memory or passage. The picture is now starting to talk to you. Your mind and body are open to hear what the Holy Spirit is saying to you through the picture.

Prayer. As the picture moves within you, allow your heart to be open to what God might be saying to you in this time of prayer. Make space for God to speak, which may come in the form of a picture in your mind, a memory, a colour or symbol. Where in your life is God calling you to act, to bring more colour or love?

Contemplation. Now close your eyes and rest in God. Become aware of your breathing once again, imaging the love of God filling you on the 'in' breath, and that love flowing out to all the world as you exhale. Allow the rhythm of your breathing to be steady and slow, and rest in God. When you are ready, slowly open your eyes and allow your gaze to fall into the room or wherever you are.

Christine Valters Paintner[39] suggests this practice is close to what the writer of the Letter to the Ephesians in the New Testament meant by 'seeing with the eyes of the heart' (Ephesians 1:18). This reminds us again of the necessary interconnectedness of our bodies, minds and emotions as *visio divina* helps us explore the meaning of photos.

Extended example – Tim Mooney's *visio divina* process

There is no one standard way of engaging in *visio divina* as an individual, but every guide breaks the process down into a number of discrete unhurried steps. We will now introduce you to another method of *visio divina*, devised by Tim Mooney, originally designed for contemplating works of art. We will then see how it has been applied to contemplation of a world-famous photo.

Tim Mooney is a Presbyterian Pastor, Spiritual Director, and Fine Artist. He is currently a Parish Associate at Central Presbyterian Church in Denver, Colorado, and was adjunct professor for the Diploma in the Art of Spiritual Direction program at San Francisco Theological Seminary, 2000-2015. His artwork can be seen at www.timmooneystudio.com.

Tim explains that *visio divina* involves slowing down, paying deep attention to an image, and allowing God to address you through the image. He says, 'it invites us to see at a more contemplative pace. It invites us to see all there is to see, exploring the entirety of the image. It invites us to see deeply, beyond first and second impressions, below initial ideas, judgments, or understandings. It invites us to be seen, addressed, surprised, and transformed by God who is never limited or tied to any image, but speaks through them.'[40]

There is no set time frame for this process of *visio divina*, but twenty to thirty minutes is recommended.

1. **Preparation** – Tim proposes that *visio divina* is best set in the context of prayer: as you begin, 'take a few moments to open your heart and mind to God'.

2. **Initial Response** – This step involves discovering your immediate raw reactions to the image, whilst keeping an open mind as to what it might eventually mean to you: 'When you are ready, slowly look and notice the image, taking your time to let feelings and thoughts come to you as you take in forms, figures, colours,

lines, textures, and shapes. What does it look like, or remind you of? What do you find yourself drawn to? What do you like and not like? What are your initial thoughts? What feelings are evoked? In this initial stage of your prayer simply notice these responses without judgment or evaluation. If you don't like the image, or the feelings evoked, simply acknowledge that this is your initial response and continue to stay open to the image and the prayer. If you have an immediate idea as to what the image means, again, simply acknowledge that this is your initial response and stay open to "the more" as the prayer unfolds.'

3. **Pondering the Image** – This step involves continuing to plumb the depths of the image and becoming more aware of some of the reasons underlying your own intellectual and visceral responses: 'As your prayer expands, return to the image with an open heart and mind. New thoughts, meanings, and feelings may arise; initial impressions may expand and deepen. Explore more fully the meanings that come to you, and the feelings associated with the image and its colours and forms. Be aware of any assumptions or expectations that you bring to the image. No matter what your response is to the image – delight, disgust, indifference, confusion – ponder prayerfully the reason for your various responses and what these responses might mean for you.'

4. **Revelation and Response** – This step involves becoming aware of anything important that is being evoked or revealed to you through the image and includes an invitation to frame a fitting response: 'As your prayer deepens, open yourself to what the image might reveal to you. What does it and the Spirit want to say, evoke, make known, or express to you as you attend to it in quiet meditation? Become aware of the feelings, thoughts, desires and meanings evoked by the image and how they are directly connected to your life. Does it evoke for you important meanings or values, remind you of an important event or season, or suggest a new or different way of being? What desires and longings are evoked in your prayer? How do you find yourself wanting to respond to what you are experiencing? Take the

time to respond to God in ways commensurate with your prayer: gratitude, supplication, wonder, lament, confession, dance, song, praise, etc.'

5. **Impact** – This step invites you to make explicit any outcomes from your *visio divina* experience that you wish to carry forward: 'In the remaining few minutes of your prayer with this image, bring to mind or jot down in a journal (whatever way is most helpful for you) the insights you want to remember, actions you are invited to take, wisdom you hope to embody, or any feelings or thoughts you wish to express.'

6. **Rest** – The *visio divina* process ends where it began, in prayer: 'bring your prayer to a close by resting in God's grace and love.'

Visio divina in practice

Tim Mooney's process is an attractive and effective way of doing *visio divina*. Spiritual director, ordained minister and writer, Julie McCarty, has used Tim's process to explore Dorothea Lange's photo, 'Migrant Mother'. This iconic image was made by renowned photographer, Dorothea Lange (1895–1965) in 1936 at a migrant farm workers camp in California, during the Great Depression.

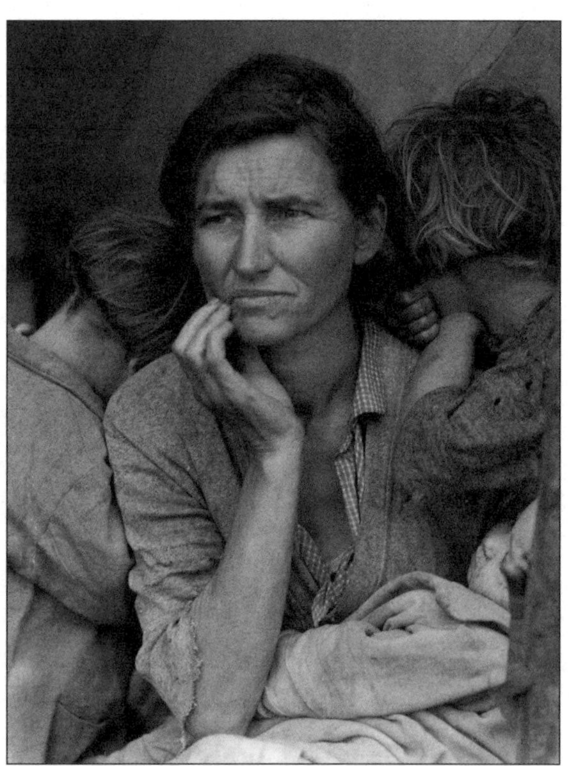

'Migrant Mother', by Dorothea Lange 1936, Library of Congress, Prints and Photographs Division, FSA/OWI Collection (Public Domain)

Julie described in her blog how *visio divina* helped her engage with this photo.[41] Whilst evidently inspired by Tim Mooney's *visio divina* method, Julie does not treat it in a rigidly formulaic way. We have numbered the following excerpts to correlate roughly with Tim's sections.

Julie said: '… just so I wouldn't have too many preconceived ideas, I looked for an image not usually found in churches, and decided upon Dorothea Lange's 1936 photograph'. She explained:

1. I set aside 20-30 minutes for the process, beginning by asking the Holy Spirit to guide my prayer.

2. I spend a little time just observing the various parts of the picture:
    a. The woman's sleeve is tattered. She has no make-up and there are wrinkles near her eyes.
    b. Why do the children hide their faces? Are they ashamed to be seen?
    c. The baby on her lap is wrapped in an oversize garment and has dirt on his or her face.
    d. The woman looks to be 40-something,'

3. I know from my reading that her name is Florence Owens Thompson, 32, married mother of seven children. In this photo, taken during the Great Depression, she is sitting in a three-sided lean-to canvas tent. These facts make me think about the economy of today and people who suffer around the world, especially the homeless, many of whom are children. I imagine the faces of other migrant women of various races and ethnicities. Would I feel the same empathy for each of them as I feel for the woman in the picture?

4. After praying for the grace to love *all* people with equal intensity, I focus my attention back on the picture once again. The woman's expression haunts me. She may be worried, but she is determined. I think she is going to do whatever it takes to feed her children. With her hand placed under her chin, she reminds

me of Rodin's bronze sculpture "The Thinker". Yes, I decide, she is indeed a strong woman, a brave woman, dead set on caring for her hungry children.

I wonder, did Mary, the mother of Jesus, ever look so strong and determined? She, too, was a "migrant mother," on the move with Joseph, first traveling as a pregnant woman to Bethlehem, then fleeing to Egypt to save her child from death, and some years later to Nazareth. Did the Holy Family ever experience hunger pangs? Surely Mary must have felt this same fierce love and deep resolve to do whatever was necessary to care for her Child.

Why have I never seen this look of strength and determination on the face of Mary in statues or paintings? Wouldn't Mary have been radically committed to do all in her power to fulfil God's will? Wouldn't her love of God have been *strong?* Are these characteristics of Mary portrayed in sacred art but I just didn't notice?

Come to think of it, wouldn't God have the same type of parental concern for us? Could we imagine the Divine Face looking something like this woman, in terms of her strength and determination? Doesn't God love us as much—no even more—than the very best of mothers?

5. Sometimes we think of Scripture as comforting, but the Word of God also challenges us to become more like Christ. I think the prayer form *visio divina* has the same potential. After the above prayer time, I observed myself feeling less whiney about my own inconveniences and more grateful. I found myself intentionally smiling at people who look "different" from me. And, when writing this post, I recalled that Hosea 13:8 compares God to a mother bear, who expresses fierceness if her cubs are threatened or taken away.'

CHAPTER 3

Letting photos speak to us

In this chapter we explore ways in which photos can help us see the world and ourselves differently. We like to call this process, 'letting photos speak to us'. Our choice of term is slightly unusual as clearly a photo does not vocalise its feelings in the way we speak to one another. Yet, photos raise emotions and memories within us and spark our imagination. By noticing these feelings, we discover that the photo has been a conversation partner and we discover new possibilities within our lives. Without the photo we would not have felt those emotions, memories, and feelings at that moment in time. Of course, a lot of our communications are non-vocal, we make judgements about people based on what is often called body language; and smells, sounds, scenes, objects or places can all evoke emotions and memories.

In her book on contemplative photography, Jan Philips suggests photos have the power to heal, at three levels.[42] The first level involves the process of taking the image, when we are absorbed in the present moment, not worrying about past or future. Philips suggests the second level of healing is found within the person being photographed, through the photographer's loving gaze. We would add that this level of healing extends to anything being photographed because to photograph something we must first notice it, and it is through noticing we are demonstrating its value through the act of paying attention to it. This could be, say, a person, a fallen leaf, or a bird in flight. The third level of healing happens when we look at the photo we have taken, which may move us and connect us with our emotions. It is this third level we are primarily considering in this chapter when we ask the question; how do photos speak to us? We would want to add a fourth level of healing to Philips' three, which is the ability of photos to heal as we share them with another person. As we talk about the picture with others and also listen to them describing what they see, how it moves them and what they feel, we are learning to see life as each other experiences it. This process deepens our connectedness with one another. It can be a place of healing because understanding helps to promote mutual understanding. It is powerful to look at photos on your own, but always consider sharing them with another person. Later in our book we explore in more depth the power of sharing photos.

Whilst our focus in this chapter is on the photo and how it can speak to us, whether that is in its printed or digital form, we will suggest some ways in which we can photograph things to produce those photos. As Philips' view of photography reminds us, the healing power of photos is linked to the taking of photos and we feel it is helpful to keep in mind the process of creating an image as we later view that image. We hope you our reader will forgive this slight blurring of boundaries within this chapter. We will draw on some basic photographic understanding of light alongside some ancient practices, such as St Ignatius's Examen, to explore how these can be used and adapted to allow photos to speak to us. Each section is divided into first a short reflection, followed by a suggested exercise. Feel free to adapt our exercises so they work for you.

Placing the present in the context of the past

We often think of the past in terms of things which happened a long time ago, often before we were born. Within this section, our main focus is on using images, taken within our lifetime, to reflect on our personal past and present. But before we explore the recent past, we feel it is important to acknowledge the more distant

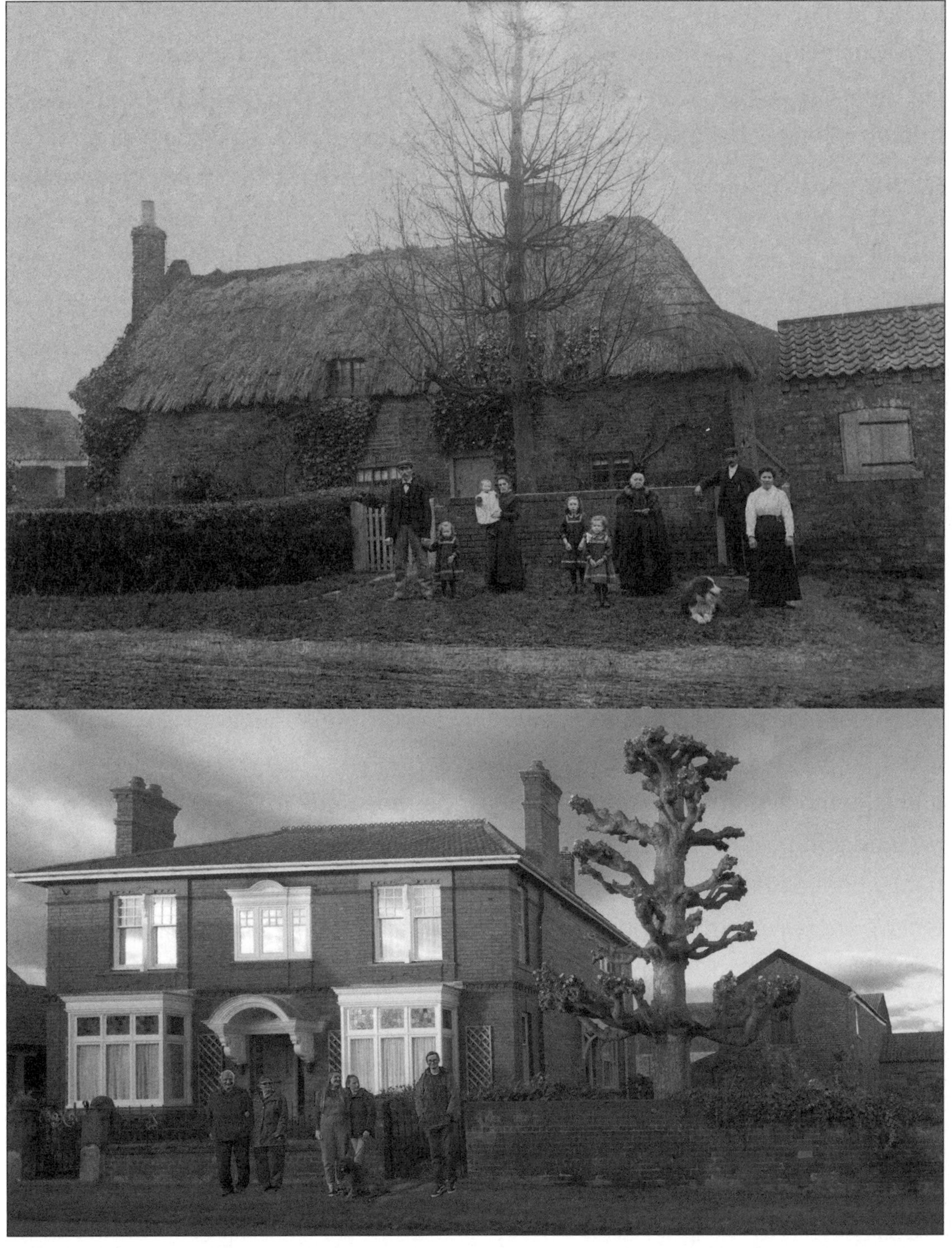

The Sycamore Tree © Andy Lindley

past and that many of us will have access to historical photos, like these of Andy's family home, past and present. Over 120 years divide the juxtaposed photos, and yet there is a continuity of family kinship and the presence of the same sycamore tree, amid huge changes to their family home. Such photos speak to a larger story and sense of belonging and help us discern our place in relation to the generations that have gone before us, and without whom we would not be here today. Like the rootedness of the sycamore tree in these pictures, we can have a sense of our identity and place in the world, remembering all those who have played a part in our life, both those we knew and perhaps those we never met, and preserving both happy and more challenging memories. Our world and our story contain the stories of many others. When we look at our own photos, such as the pictures of Andy's family home, it can be helpful to pause and reflect on how the people in those pictures have helped shape the person we are today, and consider how their values and example may live on through our own lives.

In modern society photos are such a big part of our lives, from portraits hanging on the wall to the wedding albums we may share with children and grandchildren, from our social media feeds to the pictures we look at in books and magazines, that we do not stop to think that in many ways photos are strange things. Photos are a two-dimensional digital or physical representation which holds a memory from a unique moment in time which will never be repeated, Yet, they have the power to bring that past event into the present moment. When we look at a picture of a happy time on holiday with friends, a birthday party, or a nature walk, we almost feel we are reliving that experience once again as we laugh and reminisce. We can sometimes feel as if a person pictured is in the room with us. When we look at a picture we often talk as if we are back in that moment of time the picture was created. This can be accentuated if we look at 3D stereoscopic images, which can give us a strong sense of immersion in another place and time.

Mindfulness practice encourages us to focus on the present moment, as this is the only place we can inhabit – the past has been, and the future is yet to come. Lacking the science fiction invention of time machines, we can never inhabit past or future and an undue worry about either of these places can have a detrimental effect on our mental health. Yet, photos connect us with, and encourage us to revisit, a past event. One of the reasons mindfulness encourages us to live in the present moment is because the way in which we inhabit the present will impact how we view the past and meet the future. The biblical scholar Meg Warner, in her book on the life of Joseph, explores the importance of being able to tell and reframe our story in order to recover from any mental trauma and build our resilience to face life's challenges.[43] As we tell the story of our life it is a story of the past and photos play an important role in helping us tell and shape that life story. This impacts how we will continue to live out and develop that story into the future.

As we have mentioned, when we talk about the past, we tend to think of something that happened quite a long time ago, yet your reading of this sentence is already in the past. This is the recent-past and within this section we will especially think about ways of engaging with your recent past. To help with our exploration we turn to some of the teachings of a sixteenth-century Christian mystic, a monk called St Ignatius of Loyola. St Ignatius founded an Order who today are known as the Jesuits and a core belief St Ignatius held was that God can be found in all things. This idea is important within contemplative photography as it means we can potentially find God in each photo we look at. It also suggests that everything we look at whilst we are in the process of photographing contains something precious and unique. Put another way, it means God is to be found in the present moment of taking a picture, as well as our reflection on the past when we look at a photo.

One of the exercises St Ignatius taught his followers is known as the 'examen'. Essentially St Ignatius is asking his followers regularly to reflect on the events which have occurred in the past few hours or entire day, and place these in the context of the present moment of their reflection. In doing this we recognise how God was present in the events of the day within the hours that have now past, and how this impacts the present moment that will lead into the future. This is similar to the process that looking at a picture creates. A picture can only ever reflect a past event, but as we gaze at it that past event is brought into the present moment. Perhaps had the camera been invented in the time of St Ignatius he would have used photos in his examen. Certainly, modern monks, such as the Trappist, Thomas Merton, have used the camera as an aid to contemplation. The examen is a short reflective prayer designed to be used several times throughout the day to help people remember God's presence in all that they do. For St Ignatius these reflections are the most important parts of the day because these moments of reflection and thankfulness affect every other moment. Psychological research consistently demonstrates the importance of thankfulness for our wellbeing, so this reflective prayer can help us live more effectively. It is important to remember that to be thankful does not seek to deny the painful and difficult experiences which also form a part of life. Christian belief does not seek to deny these painful parts of life, but believes God walks alongside us in both the good and more challenging times.

Today many Christians use this prayer at the end of each day before they fall asleep – a time to reflect on the day which has just passed. If you look on the Internet you will find several models and suggestions of how the examen can be practised. We believe that the camera you carry around with you can be a great way to engage with the ancient practice of the examen, because of the capacity for photos to bring the past into the present moment.

To use the camera as an aide for the examen reflective prayer, you will need to make a commitment to take some pictures throughout your day. Remembering to do this can be quite difficult so we suggest below a few ideas which can act as a prompt. Try them out and see if one works for you. You will probably think of lots more ways, so use any practice which will work for you, or mix and match our suggestions below.

Exercise: One thing you can do is to set a timer on your watch or on your phone for every two to three hours. Each time the timer beeps, pause and take a picture wherever you find yourself at that moment.

A second idea is to take a picture each time you change tasks within the day. This can be relatively easy or harder, depending on your job or lifestyle, and certainly this may not work for everyone. Christian monks

believe that the most important times of the day can be the times between tasks. We often rush through these moments without thinking, but by committing to take a picture as you change task you will bring momentary pauses throughout your day, and this can bring a greater awareness and intentionality about the task to which you are moving.

A third idea is more random, simply take a picture when you think about it. If you tend to take several pictures throughout the day anyway this could be a great technique. It is always best not to over complicate things, especially if the previous two suggestions really would not work for you.

A final idea, and one of our favourites, is to notice how you are feeling throughout the day and learn to become aware of the times you feel stressed or anxious. Within mindfulness this is often referred to as bodily awareness. There will be times for all of us within each day when we feel anxious, and we can identify these times by noticing our bodies and our thought processes. Within our bodies we can observe physical symptoms such as: slightly shallower breathing or shortness of breath, headaches, sweating, muscle tension, feeling tired, raised heartbeat, or dry mouth. Mentally we can notice within ourselves: worrying about the past or future, imagining the worst, not concentrating, racing thoughts, or being irritable. However, there can be other reasons for these mental and physical characteristics and if they become debilitating you should talk to a medical professional. Within your day if you become aware that you are anxious, stop and look at something in front of you. It doesn't have to be anything profound, just the first thing that catches your attention — even something as ordinary as the crisp packet still sitting on your desk from the rushed lunch you ate there. Notice how the light plays on what you are looking at; notice the texture, where the shadows fall and how this creates patterns and shape. Now take a picture of it. Stress and anxiety are often caused by worrying about future or past events, and one of the best ways to manage stress is to focus on the present moment. The process we have just described has centred you in the present moment without you having to think about it. Of course, you can equally use this technique around times of joy and celebration — when you feel especially happy or grateful, take a picture.

Having used one of the above techniques, or another technique which works for you, you will end your day with a photo record of the day. Each of the pictures you have taken will locate you in the past and remind you of specific things at that point within your day. Your pictures will remind you where you were, what you were doing and what you were feeling at that moment in time. You can now use these pictures to reflect on your day using an adaptation of St Ignatius's 'examen' daily prayer technique. As you are likely to be reviewing your pictures on a smartphone or tablet and screen time immediately before bed can disrupt our sleep patterns, we recommend you set aside a few minutes to do this at least two hours before you intend to go to bed.

First, become aware of God's presence with you, or the presence of others, or our interconnectedness with nature. Calm your mind by focusing on your breathing. You are not trying to control your breathing but be aware of the breaths you draw into your body and those you exhale — you share this air with all living things. Ask God to bring clarity to your day — it can at first seem a bit of a jumble!

Next, scroll through your pictures and review your day with gratitude. Notice the things you were doing, the work you did, the people you interacted with, the joys and delights, the challenges and difficulties. Pay attention to the small things, as well as the larger things, such as the food you ate or things you saw which seemed insignificant. Are there also things in your picture you did not notice at the time of taking the picture?

As you look at your pictures, scrolling back and forward, pay attention to your emotions. St Ignatius believed we can detect the presence of God's Spirit through the movements of our emotions. Reflect on those feelings, such as boredom, elation, resentment, compassion, anger, or confidence. What might God be saying through these feelings, or what can you learn about yourself through these feelings?

You will probably find one picture will jump out at you. When you feel drawn to a picture in this way, stop scrolling and allow yourself to gaze on this single picture. How were you feeling when this picture was taken — were you feeling positive or negative? What does the picture show? It may be an encounter with another, or a vivid moment of pleasure, tension or peace. It could be something which seems rather insignificant. If prayer is helpful to you, pray about these things, allowing the prayer to arise within you spontaneously. If prayer is not helpful, reflect and be aware of these things. As you pray or reflect it can be helpful to write your thoughts down.

Finally reassure yourself that you are all right. You have reached the end of the day. This can help us look forward to tomorrow with thankfulness, seeing life as a gift. Pay attention to your feelings for tomorrow. What are your hopes and desires for tomorrow, for yourself, and the people and any animals who play a part in your daily life? What are your feelings around the situations you will encounter? Are you cheerful, apprehensive, doubtful? Again, it can be helpful to write some of these feelings down.

This prayerful reflection can be a helpful discipline, regardless of how we are feeling about life and our mood. There can be times when even getting out of bed is a struggle, and perhaps managing to clean our teeth, having a shower or getting dressed are big achievements. If this is where you feel you are, then photograph the tube of toothpaste or the clothes lying on your bed, waiting to be put on, or the shower head. At other times different things will be significant, such as finishing an essay for your studies, closing a deal at work, or helping at the local food bank. The power of this reflection is it reminds us to celebrate everything; whether it seems small or large it has equal value. It also reminds us that we are not alone. For those who share a faith in the divine, it reminds us that God goes before us and walks alongside us in all our encounters. Equally, when we look at the pictures, we are reminded about the people, friends, animals, and nature which we encounter and our interconnectedness with all these things. For example, a picture of a plant on a windowsill reminds us that it shares the same air as we do, or a picture of toothpaste might remind us of the person who sold it to us.

Hold this reflection technique lightly. If you feel able to discipline yourself to take several pictures throughout the day and then spend a few minutes at the end of your day to reflect on these images, we think you will be surprised at the things you can be thankful for within your life and the hope this releases for the future.

Re-encountering places and moments of spiritual significance through your standout images

It is worth asking yourself what you believe makes a standout image. Is it an image which wins a competition? Is it an image which attracts lots of likes and positive comments when shared on a social media platform? Is it an image which brings back memories of a happy time and place? Is it an image which is technically perfect in its use of light and composition? Is it an image which makes us pause? Is it an image which gives rise to an emotional response within us?

There are many more questions which might help us explore what a standout image is, but your own answers to the above questions will help you start to understand what a standout image is to you. It is worth chatting about these

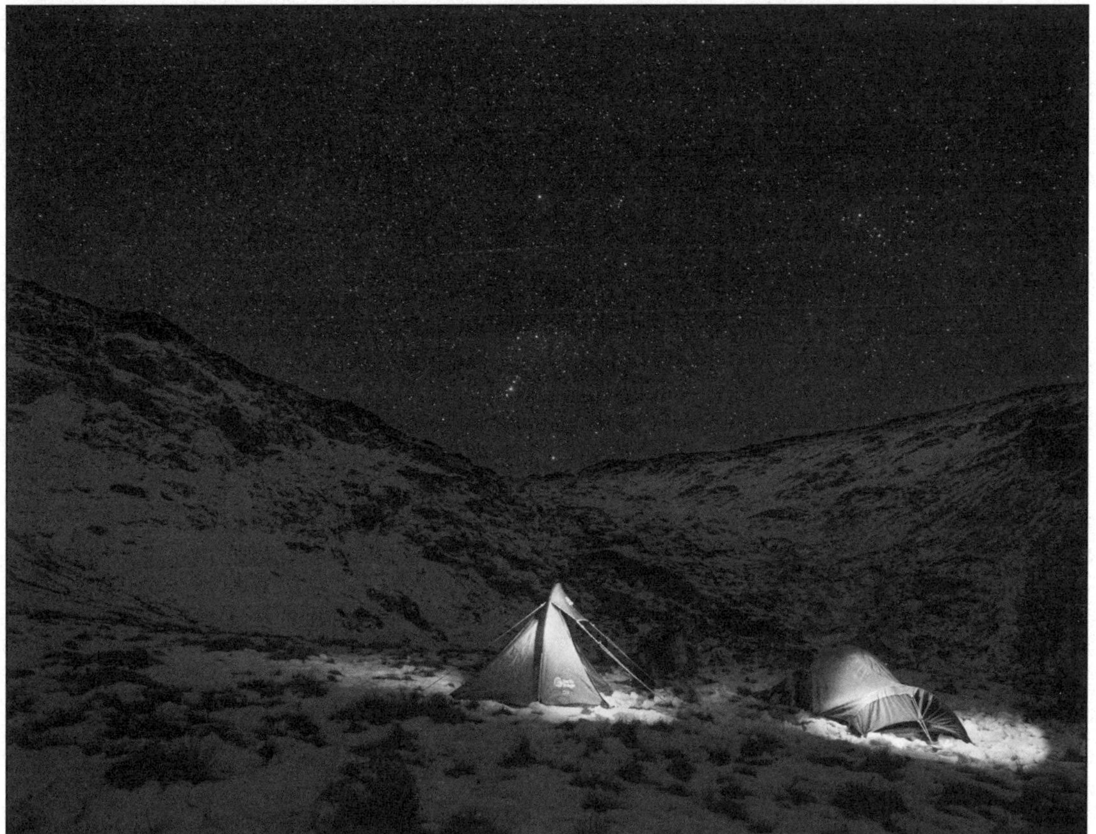

Night Sky on Harter Fell © Stephen Radley

thoughts with a friend or family member, someone you trust, as understandings can be quite different and hearing a different perspective will enlarge and inform our own. We are focusing here on standout images that help us re-encounter times and places of special spiritual significance.

What though is a moment of spiritual significance, and indeed what is spirituality? There is no one easy answer to this question as spirituality in its modern usage is quite a broad term but it is generally acknowledged to include a sense of something bigger than ourselves. It can also include asking questions that lead to a search for meaning in life, such as what does it mean to be me and to have the gift we call life? Spirituality can often be linked to questions we might have about ourselves and our identity, how we see our place within the world. Some may see spirituality as a deep sense of connectedness and that can include connection to the divine. Meaning and connectedness can be found through our relationships, our understanding of God, or through our love of art and nature.

The US doctor, Christina Puchalski who is the founder and director of the George Washington Institute for Spirituality and Health, defines spirituality as that 'aspect of humanity that refers to the way individuals seek and express meaning and purpose and the way they experience their connectedness to the moment, to self, to others, to nature, and to the significant or sacred.'[44]

The idea within this definition, that spirituality encompasses the experience of our connectedness with the present moment, is important. According to Puchalski, this aspect of our humanity – connection to the present moment – is spiritual. Sometimes our minds like to try and convince us that we can live in the past or future. We may dwell on a past event or be anxious about something which might happen in the future, but our lived reality is that we can only ever live in the present moment. As we have already noted, the past has been, and the future is yet to come.

Paradoxically, although a photo records a past event, a unique unrepeatable moment, when we hold that photograph today the past is brought into our present moment. The Canadian psychologist and one of the early pioneers of phototherapy, Judi Weiser, describes photos as 'footprints of our minds, mirrors of our lives, reflections from our hearts, frozen memories we can hold in silent stillness in our hands – forever, if we wish. They document not only where we have been but also point to where we might be going, whether we know it yet or not. We should converse with them often and listen well to the secrets their lives can tell.'[45]

Our standout images are not necessarily those which are technically perfect, or those that attract lots of likes from our friends on social media. They are images in which we are reminded of our connection with the past in the present moment. But, more than this, they also remind us of the ways in which we find meaning within our lives. Significant events might include time spent with friends, holidays to new places, exams we have passed, births of our children, managing to dress or clean our teeth in the morning (when life feels overwhelming), a flower that made us pause, or a sunset that took our breath away. The picture at the start of this section reminds Steve of a special night spent camping in the Southern Lake District with his nephew.

Training in photography can help us effectively tell our story in photos through the way we use light, moment and composition, but it can also be a hindrance in that we may fail to see the significance of a picture we deem to be technically poor. Steve tells a story of a wedding he photographed. He had taken the couple off for fifteen minutes to capture some portraits of the bride and groom. There are lots of emotions on a wedding day and this time after the ceremony can be a chance for the couple to relax for a few moments by themselves. Steve had set his lights up and he took some portraits which the couple were happy with and were technically good. Then, the groom noticed a fallen tree to one side, and he and his wife jumped on it and a few more photos followed. Steve had not had time to reposition the lights for these images which were quite spontaneous. Looking at them later he was not happy with them from a technical perspective, and nearly did not include them in the couple's gallery. Fortunately, he did and one of these pictures turned out to be the couple's favourite. Steve later asked a more experienced photographer why the couple had preferred what his training told him was a less than perfect image. His friend explained that the image contained an important memory for them: a time when they could finally relax after the feelings of anxiety which can sometimes be present earlier in the wedding day. This picture contained a key memory and reflected their fun-loving personalities and more importantly, how they connected with the present in that moment of time. Several years later Steve knows this is a picture that is proudly framed and sits on their sideboard, so that each morning, as they walk from the bedroom to the kitchen it is one of the first things they see; it acts as a prompt to remind them of that significant day in their lives and, as such, this is one of that couple's standout images.

It is important to remember that not all significant moments in our lives are of happy memories such as the one we describe above, but all our experiences in life help to shape us. As we saw earlier in the Introduction, Steve draws on how his troubling experiences of war have acted to shape the person he is today and have enlarged his appreciation of life.

Exercise: Find a place to sit quietly and think about your life, considering the times that have been significant in bringing you to the place you find yourself today. Now look through your own back-catalogue of images, you may even like to dust off an old album and find an image from one of those significant times. Judy Weiser suggests that pictures are 'footprints of the mind'. Can you remember how you felt when that picture was taken? What were your hopes and dreams at that time? Can you see how these feelings act as footprints of the mind which have helped you travel to where you are today?

Now consider Christina Puchalski's view of spirituality we quoted above. In what ways has the significant moment depicted in the photo you are looking at helped you express meaning and purpose in your life? How has it helped you experience your connectedness to the present moment, to self, to others, to nature, and to the significant or sacred? You may find it helpful to write down your answers to some of these questions in a journal which you can add to and look back on. It is often helpful to talk about them with someone you trust.

You may like to print and display your picture somewhere you will see it each day. Notice how your thoughts and feelings develop over time as you look at this picture each day. Our standout images are the ones which have acted as footprints of the mind, and they may also offer us some guidance to our future decisions and the path we will travel.

Revealing patterns of change in the light of constancy

A pattern is a design in which colours, forms, lines and shapes are repeated. The repetition can be regular or irregular. In life there is something comforting about what we often call patterns of behaviour. These are habits and things we do on a regular basis. Perhaps we always start our day with a bowl of porridge. We probably have a favourite magazine or newspaper we read and tend not to digress too far from these publications. Patterns can help keep us safe. Before a pilot takes off, they have a checklist to complete, and these checks are repeated at the beginning of each day or before each flight. When we drive to a friend's house or our place of work, we often have a favourite route, and we are unlikely to divert from this route as it is familiar and known to us.

In art, patterns can be both simple and quite complex, they can be both regular and irregular. Patterns are fun to photograph as they are to be found everywhere and can bring a unique compositional element to your photo. Typically, patterns are a repetition of tones, lines, shapes, or colours. Patterns are very common within nature. Some are obvious like the petals on a flower or the ripples on a pond flowing out from where a stone was thrown; others we might not immediately think of as patterns, such as the gentle lapping of waves as they roll onto a beach, or the regularity of ripples on a river caused by the wind blowing across it. Patterns can be made by people, nature and animals. The regular flow of bricks in a wall, the architecture in many of our ancient churches, the stacked fruit on a market stall,

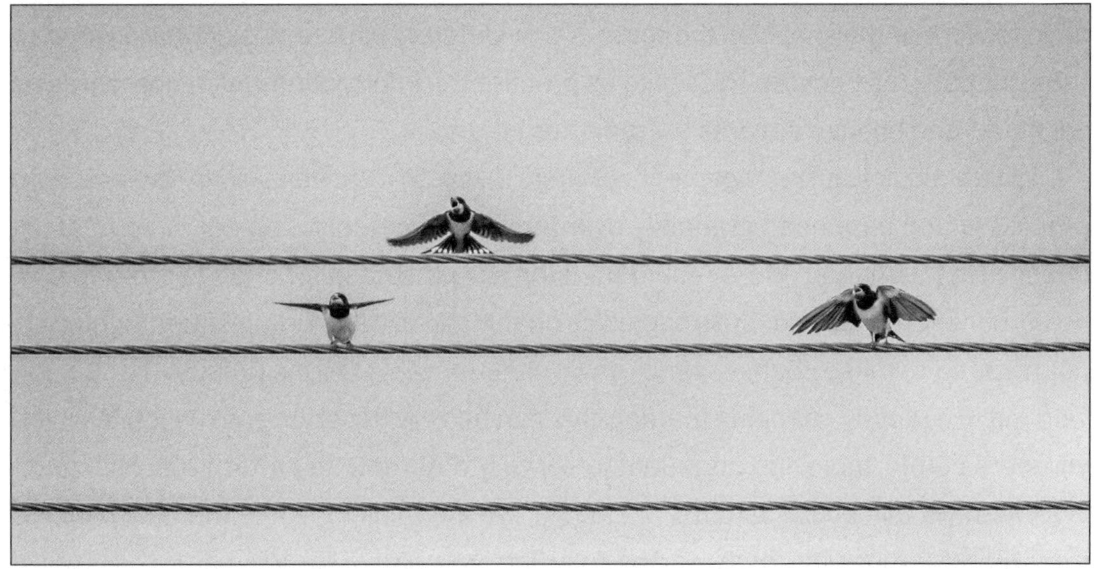

Swift Exit © Stephen Radley

the regular pattern of the twigs woven within a bird's nest or the ripples in the sand after the tide has flowed out are all patterns. In a moment we will think a little more about tonal patterns which are formed within the play of light and shadow.

As we are thinking about patterns of change, we will consider the nature of change before exploring tonal shadows in more depth. By contrast to the security we often find within patterns, change can be unsettling to us. It breaks our familiar patterns and the ways we behave which bring us feelings of comfort and safety. When something changes there can be a kind of bereavement process, as something which was familiar to us has been lost. Even a happy and long sought-after change like the birth of a baby evokes losses – some of our freedom, sleep, the intimate time we have available to spend with a partner, for example. Research shows that moving to a new house is one of the most stressful things we can do. Sometimes the move may not have been what we wished for, perhaps triggered by the end of a relationship and such stress is understandable. However, the stress is still present even if the move is something we have sought, something we have looked forward to, perhaps worked hard to achieve. But when we move, whatever the driving reason, all our patterns have been disrupted and this is challenging for us. The furniture, the pots, the bedrooms and even the kitchen are in different places. You must consciously think about your drive to work or the shops as the route is now different. Our brains are hard wired to seek out patterns because this helps us process the information which bombards us each day, and change disrupts these patterns.

Within business management, change used to be seen as an evolutionary process which happened gradually over time as an organisation adjusted to small changes in the market. More recent thinking sees the need for change often to be a revolutionary process because society is changing fast, and organisations which do not respond to these changes quickly will not survive, yet alone prosper. For people working in a rapidly changing market, this can be very unsettling as the job in which you were comfortable and confident looks very different. Its pattern has changed.

When we talk about patterns of change, we are thinking about the new patterns that emerge through the losses and gains which are a part of life. We may be hard wired to look for patterns and seek security in those patterns which we hope will not change, but paradoxically change is the one constant in life. That change might be the death of a loved one, moving into a new house, the birth of a child, redundancy from our place of work, an accident, the joy of graduating with our first degree, a new job, passing an apprenticeship and many more things, all of which contribute to the rich pattern of life.

The shadow is a constantly changing pattern we find within the natural world. It is an area of diffused light representing the shape of the object or person that has interrupted the light. As such, it is a pattern which is constantly changing, thanks to the movement of the sun in the sky and the movement of clouds which diffuse its light. Indoors, shadows change as we turn lights on and off or close and open curtains. Shadows are formed through the interplay of light and darkness, and it is this interplay which brings mystery, shape and texture. Photographers do not see darkness as a negative thing, but simply an aspect of light. Within the Judeo-Christian creation story, God creates light out of darkness, and when we think of the change presented to us through new life – such as the birth of a child or a bird emerging from its shell, or a seed germinating – that new life was formed within darkness, be that the darkness of the womb, shell, or soil. So, darkness is a place where all life starts, and life by its vibrant nature produces change.

Photographers talk about the 'quality of light,' which at its simplest is a term to describe how defined the shadows are. You will have noticed how a sunny day produces a very rapid transition between the tonal ranges, in other words the edges of a shadow are very clearly defined alongside a lighter area. By contrast, the shadows on a cloudy day are far less defined, the change in the tonal range is more gradual. If you look very carefully, there is still a shadow, but that gradual transition from light to dark makes it far harder to see. This phenomenon yields different patterns of change: for example, one day you can walk along a path which has clearly defined shadows falling from the railings which run alongside it; then the next day, even at the same time with the sun in the same position in the sky, the path looks quite different with no shadows. Shadows affect how we view people as well. Wedding photographers often hope for a cloudy day, as shadows on faces do not produce the most flattering photos. By contrast, a producer, who is making a documentary in which they interview someone whom they want to portray as untrustworthy, may use light to cast one side of the interviewee's face in shadow. When we see people lit in this way, called 'split lighting', we tend to see them as less trustworthy. Look out for this technique next time you watch an investigative documentary or television news item interviewing someone the public rate as less trustworthy or sinister!

The change in the shadow's tonal depth, is caused by the size of the light source in relation to the subject. On a sunny day the light source is very small — we know the sun is huge but its distance from us makes it relatively quite small. This produces a rapid change in tonal value. On an overcast day, the clouds act as a giant lightbox meaning the whole sky is effectively a light source. This makes the light very big in comparison to the subject, and this means the change in tonal range, the transition from dark to light, is more gradual.

Exercise 1: Next time you experience a sunny day, spend time watching the shadows. Look at how they dance as they create patterns from a slowly moving object like a tree gently blowing in the wind. Take some photos of these shadows. On the next overcast day go back to the same place at approximately the same time and look for the shadows which will be more gradual in their tonal transition (movement from dark to lighter). Take a photo of those shadows. Spend some time looking at the two pictures you have created and ask yourself which you prefer. What are the differences and similarities? How do things look different with more defined shadows compared to less defined shadows? Why do you prefer the one you have chosen? As you look at the pictures, are you reminded of patterns of change in your own life? You may find it helpful to write about these changes, noticing how they made you feel at the time, and how you feel as you reflect on the changes now. How has change led to new patterns within your own life? How do you feel about the new patterns you have identified within your life? Share your thoughts with someone you trust. If you cannot go outside, you can do

this exercise in your house using a lamp shining on something. Then, place a sheet of white paper between the lamp and the object and notice how the shadows change because the paper acts as a big diffuser, like the clouds diffuse sunlight.

Exercise 2: Find a photo from a time in your life which led to change. We have already suggested some areas of change we experience in our lives, but our list is not exhaustive. As you look at the photo ask yourself how this event has changed your life. How do you feel about these changes now, as you look back? It can be helpful to write down your reflection and to share it with someone you trust or who was part of this change.

We have suggested a paradox, that the one constant in life is change. Within the Christian faith is a belief that God's love is constant, it does not change. Do you find this statement helpful and, if so, why? As people we look for patterns to provide safety and security. Who are those in your life who provide you with a sense of safety?

Exercise 3: Take your camera out and intentionally look for patterns and photograph them — we have suggested a few places you will find patterns. When you get home look at the pictures you have taken and, as you look at them, consider the patterns in your own life. Which are healthy and produce growth; are any unhealthy? Do you feel you need to affirm or change any patterns of behaviour in your own life?

Symbolising life's choices and enabling reflection on your choices

Many of us have sat stationary in heavy traffic on a motorway, wishing we had taken a different route. At the beginning of a journey, we make choices: should I travel along this road or that one? And those choices will have an impact on the outcome of our journey. When our journey runs smoothly, we rarely think about the choice we made. When an accident or congestion impede our progress, we find ourselves wishing we had made a different choice. Perhaps, had we looked at the traffic reports when we were planning our route, we could have made a choice which would have got us to our destination in a more timely manner. But often things change during our journey which were not apparent when we made our original choices — for instance, we had no knowledge that a lorry would shed its load and close two lanes of our motorway.

The metaphor of 'journey' is helpful when thinking about the choices we make within our lives. In a journey we must choose the direction we are going to travel and sometimes things change which may be beyond our control but mean we must move in a different direction for a time; or perhaps we continue in the same direction, just at a slower pace, as can happen on a motorway in heavy traffic. Often travelling in different directions will lead to the same destination, but what we see as we travel is quite different. If a motorway is closed, we will be diverted onto surrounding country lanes for a time, but ultimately we still reach our original destination. Sometimes, we may choose to change our destination. Similarly, our lives can take different directions, depending on the choices we make.

When we look at one of our old photos, we may begin to think about the journey we have taken in our life; the photo itself forms a part of that life journey, in that it records a place we inhabited for a time. It is a part of the story of our life which has brought us to the place where we now find ourselves. At the end of this section, we have an exercise in which we use an old photo to explore the choices we have made in life. But first, we want to explore the idea of direction and how this enables us to reflect on life's choices, through another term photographers use to describe light — the 'direction of light.'

As its name suggests, 'direction of light' describes the direction from which a light source is shining on a subject. The direction of light helps to create texture and shape in our pictures. For ease, photographers often break down the direction of light into three types: side light, front light and back light. When we look at something, it is important to notice the primary direction of the light, and, as we do this, we can become more aware of how it shapes what we are looking at.

Front lighting is often used in photography as it is quite simple to set up if you are using artificial light, and it will give quite an even illumination without any harsh shadows. A drawback with front facing light is that it creates less dramatic images, where everything looks flat and two-dimensional because shadows fall behind the subject. One of the reasons we tend to dislike our passport pictures is because front facing light must be used which produces a flat looking picture. If you have a flash mounted on your camera, facing forward, this will produce front lit images.

Because front lighting produces flat images it is rarely used in portraiture. A classic way to photograph people is with a side light which is slightly above and about 45 degrees to the side of a person. This is often the direction the sun shines on us and will tend to produce quite flattering pictures.

The directionality of light can be a helpful metaphor for life. As you learn to notice side light and use it within your photography it can be a used as a trigger to cause you to pause and reflect on who walks alongside you and the people you walk alongside. The importance of how we accompany one another through the journey of life is illustrated through a New Testament story in which the resurrected Jesus walks alongside two of his disciples on a road leading from Jerusalem to a town called Emmaus on the first Easter Day (Luke 24:13-35). The disciples had pinned all their hopes on Jesus, who had led them into Jerusalem a few days earlier, only to see him arrested and executed by the authorities. Disillusioned, they choose not to stay where Jesus had led them, instead they walk away from Jerusalem. Within the Christian story is the central belief that God conquers death through the resurrection of Jesus, and hence the resurrected Jesus joins these two disciples and talks to them, listening to their deep sadness as they walk together — in the wrong direction, away from Jerusalem. It is only when they pause to eat together that they recognise Jesus and at this point in the story they choose to rush back to Jerusalem where they will later receive the promise of the Holy Spirit. Central to this narrative is the importance of walking alongside someone. Side lighting can cause us to pause and reflect on who we walk alongside, listening and encouraging through our presence, and on who does this for us. Are we sometimes called to walk in the wrong direction with another? We mentioned that front facing light does not produce flattering images – perhaps when we find someone or a situation difficult, we simply need to, metaphorically, change the direction of the light we are using to look at that person or situation. There is always more than one perspective available in our life and light's different directions remind us of this reality.

When a light source is behind what we are looking at, it is called back-lighting. Light shining from behind creates separation from other objects in a picture and gives them a greater sense of depth. It can be fun to experiment using light from behind when taking photos, as it can create some quite dramatic shots. Back-lighting is often used in films to create a sense of mystery and drama as people appear as silhouettes with the brighter light behind. Try looking at a spider's web with the early morning dew on it and position yourself so the low morning sun is behind it. That dew can appear as fine jewels and is a reminder that even the seemingly insignificant things in our life have a great beauty when lit creatively.

Silhouettes occur because something is blocking the light. They can be dramatic to look at but also cause us to reflect on things which may block our light, and ways in which we block light from reaching others. One title ascribed to Jesus is 'Light of the World' – suggesting how the Christian faith can illuminate the way we live. There is a story about how Jesus became angry at the trading which took place in the Temple and, such was his anger, he overturned the tables of the traders to prevent their trade from continuing. The temple trade sold animals to be used in worship at exaggerated prices, meaning those who could not afford the price could feel they were kept from encountering God and that God was not interested in them. The trade acted as a barrier to people and this seems to have been at the root of Jesus' anger. As we look at a silhouette, we may reflect on whether our actions might be blocking the love of

God or fullness of life from reaching other people. This can perhaps be through hasty judgements we make which can stop us accepting and loving people as they are. This may also be through our failure to challenge an injustice. The wonderful thing about light is it only needs a small crack to enter a room, reminding us that our smallest efforts can achieve tremendous good.

Try noticing and experimenting with the different directions of light in your photography. As you move around an object that has a fixed light source you are changing the direction of its lighting. There are lots of types of light source, including such things as a lamp in a room, a window, the sun, a torch or the flash on your camera. If you are using a flash and can detach it from your camera, try positioning it in different places around the object, while you stay in the same place. Notice how the pictures look quite different. You can achieve a similar effect by shining a torch on something and moving the torch around and, taking pictures as the torch is held in different positions. If you are outside, try to note where the sun is in the sky. Even on a cloudy day the sunlight will be brighter on one side of an object. On cloudy days, you can work out where the sun is coming from by holding your hand up or a piece of white card. One side of your hand or the card will be slightly brighter, and that will tell you the direction of the sunlight.

We have framed our thinking about life's choices within the context of journey. We then suggested that noticing the direction of light as we take and look at photos can act as a metaphor to help us explore the choices and direction within our own life. We now suggest some exercises through which we can use photos to think about life's choices but we urge our readers to be compassionate to themselves and others. This reflection may remind us of choices we have made which we feel were good and facilitated growth, but it may also remind us of choices we feel have caused hurt to ourselves or others. It can also remind us of choices we had little control over and, again, these can be choices which have facilitated growth or hurt. All our choices have the capacity to teach us new things, and we take this new knowledge into our future choices. We can never change the start of a journey, but we can aim to change the end. One of the greatest things we do in life is to continue our journey, whether that is through small stumbling steps or giant strides, through what we consider good choices as well as those with hindsight we may consider to have been poorer choices. All of our choices help us grow as people and tell us more about ourselves and our world.

Exercise 1. Early in their studies, every student on a photography course is likely to be given a picture by their tutor and told to work out in which direction the light is shining. When shadows are clearly defined this is quite easy, but where the shadows are less obvious this becomes harder. Often there can be more than one light source, so a subject is lit from several directions which lifts shadows. Each source of light helps to creates the shape and texture in the photo, but one of those sources will be the most dominant.

Try this exercise for yourself. Look through your photos, choose one and then spend some time looking at it. Notice the shadows in the photo, both the larger shadows and smaller ones which show texture. Notice how the direction of light defines and gives a sense of shape. Do you feel the way the image is lit is complimentary to the subject; or is it lit like a passport photo, not the most complimentary way to light something? Why do you feel the way the image is lit, the direction the light is shining on it, is, or is not, complimentary? As you look at the photo, consider if there is something in your life which you find difficult? Imagine that this is the subject of one of your photos. Is there another way you can look at this situation? Can you shine the light of your pattern of thoughts and feelings on it from a different direction which will make it look quite different? Is there someone in your life you find difficult? Is there another direction you can shine the light of your pattern of thoughts and feelings which will allow you to see that person differently? Do you see the best in yourself? If not, is there another way you can shine the light of your pattern of thoughts and feelings on yourself to see yourself differently? It might be helpful to write down your thoughts on these questions. If you get stuck, look back at your original picture.

Exercise 2. Find a picture of yourself that was taken 5 or 10 years ago. As you look at the picture, write a letter to your younger self. What would you say to this person about the choices they are going to make, and the direction those choices have led them. What are the things which have been difficult and made your journey harder, what are the things you feel have been less difficult and made your journey smoother? Are there different ways you can direct the light of your thoughts and feelings as you consider the harder and smoother parts of your life journey? Be gentle to yourself as you do this, remind yourself that you try your best and this is all anyone can ever do. Our decisions and experiences make us wiser and we learn more about ourselves through the choices we make. Such learning helps us to 'live life in all its fullness' — the abundant life Jesus wished for his followers (John 10:10).

Within Christian faith there is a belief that God accompanies us throughout life, which means God is there alongside every choice we make. How does that knowledge make you feel as you look at that picture of your younger self?

Revealing colour and expressing emotion

We have looked at two of the properties of light, which photographers should always consider before taking a picture — its quality and direction. We are now going to consider a third property, that of colour.

There is something beautiful about the simplicity of black and white photography, the removal of colour allows us to see the quality and direction of light more easily. However, a good black and white photographer is also very aware of the colour present in the scene being photographed, as, once converted to black and white, these colours have a huge impact on the tonal range within the final photo. Colour is one of light's most amazing gifts to us and has a capacity to evoke so many different feelings and emotions. The emotional responses associated with colour cover a large spectrum; some responses are obvious, some perhaps less so. Some emotional responses are universal and rooted in our human anatomy or natural features; others tend to be linked to a specific culture, country or region. The marketing industry knows the power of colour to evoke a response within us. Have you noticed the colours predominantly used for different types of products?

Many people feel especially drawn to the light at the beginning and end of each day which is often marked by a procession of colour through the sky – from 'golden hour' to 'blue hour' at sunset and vice versa at dawn. Depending on whether you are a night owl or a lark, you may prefer one or other. Sunset and sunrise are often described as 'thin places' in Celtic spirituality, a time when we experience the spiritual and physical overlapping as one. The colours visible at these times of the day demonstrate how colour can arise at the meeting of light and darkness. This is an idea which is explored in detail by the physicist, Arthur Zajonc, in his book, *Catching the Light: The entwined history of light and mind*.[46] As we mentioned earlier, new life grows within darkness, and it is after the growth and rest of night that a blaze of colour heralds the start of a new day. The renowned seventeenth-century physicist, Isaac Newton, first discovered that the white light we see is a combination of parent colours twisted into one. We only see those parent colours when an object reflects that one colour, or the density of the atmosphere allows us to see the slower wavelengths of that parent colour. When light is refracted into its separate colours by a prism or by water droplets, we see a rainbow. It is a curious fact that to observe a rainbow in the sky we must turn our back on the primary light source, usually the sun. Within Judeo-Christian tradition the rainbow is seen as a symbol of hope, promise and trust.[47] The way in which a rainbow combines the visible colours of light has seen it used in wider society to symbolize equality and hope, and it has been used by a variety of movements, such as those working for peace, national reconstruction, healthcare and the LGBTQ+ community.

The twelfth-century mystic, Hildegard of Bingen used the classical Latin word *viriditas*, which means 'greenness', within her spirituality. To Hildegard this word described the greening power of God, that life force which brings forth growth. This greening power was inherent 'in all the beautiful things of this world'.[48] Hildegard advised her readers to: 'Glance at the sun. See the moon and the stars. Gaze at the beauty of earth's greenings. Now, think what delight God gives to humankind with all these things.'[49] Interestingly, Hildegard used a colour to represent both physical and spiritual awakening: this colour is another 'thin place' where the distance between the material and spiritual is tissue thin. Green is of course the most common colour in nature. Within the Christian tradition, green is often used to represent creation, and is the colour of altar frontals in parish churches within the Anglican and Catholic traditions for most of the year.

Film makers know the power of colour. The 1970s children's television programme which followed the life of a cat called Bagpuss always started in black and white. At the beginning of each episode Bagpuss is woken, and, as his eyes open, the scene changes to colour, representing the opportunities the new day will bring. A similar technique is used in the film *The Wizard of Oz*. The film starts in black and white but when Dorothy is transported to the land of Oz everything turns to colour. When she returns to her home in Kansas, she finds that place is now filled with colour, representing the new life and opportunities her adventures in Oz have taught her to see in her homeland.

Emotions tend to be linked to different colours. Red is a colour of warmth, love, fire, anger, strength, passion, and blood. The designer and colour theorist Faber Birren describes this colour as the most ardent hue of the colour spectrum and notes how it is linked to opposites in human behaviour: saint and the sinner, patriotism and anarchy, love and hatred, compassion and war.[50] Throughout history we see red used to represent majesty, triumph and royalty. It is an emotionally intense colour.

Green is a quite different colour to red, but is generally seen as complementary to red – think of holly and berries at Christmas and how the two colours often appear together in nature. Green gives rise to feelings of freshness, mystery, and hope. It contains feelings of light and coolness, cheer and restraint. As we have already noted, green is an important colour within Christianity and represents creation. It is the most restful colour to the human eye. Jewellers used to have an emerald on their desk which they would look at to rest their eyes from the intense visual work of their trade. Green is a colour of safety and tells us it is safe to proceed at traffic lights; and products such as green energy promise power which does not damage our environment.

When we think of yellow, we often imagine sunlight. This means we often associate it with cheerfulness and springtime and summer. It is a warm colour which draws our attention, and sits alongside red as one of the most visible colours to the human eye. Taxis in New York are painted yellow for this reason. Although it arouses feelings of cheerfulness, when placed against black it can be used to provide a warning. Many of us feel a note of panic when we see the black and yellow markings on a wasp or hornet.

Blue is felt as a cool colour, denoting formality, and is often associated with knowledge and serenity. Like green we often associate blue with nature, as it is the colour of the sky, ocean and sea. Blue can often have a calming effect on your mind and body. Within Christian art it is often associated with truth, loyalty, compassion and purity. Mary, the Mother of Jesus, has been traditionally depicted dressed in blue, at least from the twelfth century, using the precious pigment ultramarine.[51]

The marketing industry knows how colour impacts our emotions and uses this knowledge to great effect. We all like to believe we are not influenced by marketing, but an interesting exercise is to search images on the Internet with a search string such as: 'natural products', 'health products' or 'medical products'. You will be surprised at the uniformity of colours within the images being promoted by different businesses. Colour can help inform the way we see the world in which we live and, just like Dorothy found in *The Wizard of Oz*, it can open our eyes to new opportunities and possibilities present within our life.

Steve tells of a birthday trip his wife had arranged to the Shard skyscraper in London. Timed to be there over sunset, Steve was looking forward to the colours which could be photographed across the London skyline from this high vantage point. As the train pulled into London, thick clouds descended over the city. Arriving at the Shard thirty minutes later, heavy rain was beating onto the streets. The clouds never lifted, everything from high up looked grey and there was no sunset to be seen. However, as darkness descended, the city lit up with amazing colours, beautifully reflected along the line of the River Thames.

In Steve's daytime images of the Shard there is little feeling and looking at them you can sense the disappointment Steve felt. Those taken after night had fallen are completely different. The colours brought a connectedness for Steve to the place he was photographing. Ideally, we should always feel involved in what we frame through the viewfinder. As we suggested in the Introduction, in contemplative photography you should never have a prior image in mind but rather allow the image to find you and treasure this gift.

Exercise. Find some time in your day when you can intentionally photograph colour. You might be able to use a lunch break, but all you require is about 15 minutes. If you are using your phone camera, you may find it helpful to put it on airplane mode to avoid distractions. Now sit somewhere quiet and close your eyes. With your eyes closed, allow a colour to flood your imagination — this is your colour, the one which has chosen you. Now open your eyes and go for a short walk, walking slowly and intentionally. As you walk, look for your colour, the colour that chose you when you had your eyes closed a moment ago. When you find something with your colour, spend time just looking at it. Write down how you feel or any words that come to mind. Next, photograph it in different ways (close, distant, low down, etc.). Use the rest of the time you have available to notice other objects which contain your colour and photograph them.

In the evening, look at the colour photos you took on your walk. As you look at your photos, use the following questions to explore them and your emotions: What emotions do you feel as you look at the photos you have created? Are these emotions different to the ones you felt and noted down when you took the picture? Can you describe why you chose that particular

colour? Does this tell you anything about your life? Do you notice these emotions in other areas of your life — what might this be saying to you? Do you see anything different from what you originally saw? If so, what do you feel these changes are saying to you? It can be helpful to write these thoughts down as well, and we always encourage you, if you feel able, to share your thoughts with someone you trust.

Finding beauty in the ordinary

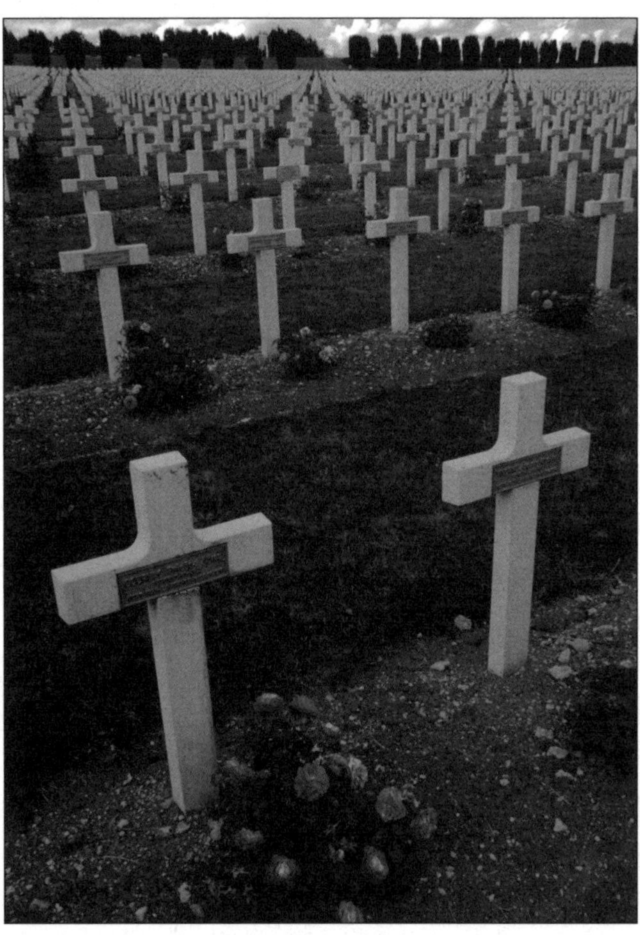

We include this section with a little trepidation as many great scholars have explored the theme of beauty which is multifaceted and is a complex philosophical idea. Ideas of beauty have not always focused on aesthetic attractiveness as they do today and have, instead, included ideas such as truth and character. In modern society we can have a narrow definition of what constitutes beauty and a whole cosmetics and health industry has grown up to ensure our bodies conform to this definition.

War Graves © Andy Lindley

We recognise there are injustices within our world which lead to suffering in many forms, and such suffering cannot be described as beautiful, nor do we want to deny its existence. Our hope is that through the careful use of the camera our eyes may be opened to the challenges of the world, and our hearts moved to act in small ways to address those challenges – and such action does perhaps contain at least a sliver of beauty. There is however a danger that our focus can be purely on suffering and for some reason our eyes can be drawn to this. Someone who works in journalism once told Steve they had a saying, 'if it bleeds, it reads'. Whilst we should not ignore that which is not beautiful in our world, if our focus is on suffering only, we can fail to see the far greater good in the world.

From earliest Christianity, God has been described as 'beautiful' and has even sometimes been equated with 'beauty' itself – ultimate beauty, that is, alongside God's ultimate truth, wisdom and goodness. One of the Psalms from the Hebrew Bible speaks of contemplating God's beauty: 'One thing I asked of the Lord, that will I seek after: to live in the house of the Lord all the days of my life, to behold the beauty of the Lord' (Psalm 27:4 NRSV). Christians believe that the beauty of the Trinity is reflected in the wondrous world that God has created. As the Christian mystic and social activist, Simone Weil (1909-1943), put it: 'The Beauty of the world is Christ's tender smile for us coming through matter. He is really present in the universal beauty.'[52] The beauty of God can also be reflected in the beautiful and graceful lives of those closest to God: individuals who show moral and spiritual beauty, sometimes described as 'the beauty of holiness' (Psalm 29:3 AV). The Jesuit, Gerard Manley Hopkins, spoke in one of his poems of 'God's better beauty, grace.'[53]

Sometimes photographers and artists depict scenes of ugliness that seem far away from a world of beauty or the beauty of God. Photography has not always sought to create beautiful images, indeed, in the history of photography, there have been strong reactions against beautiful photography. For instance, the Pictorialist movement (c. 1869-1915) – which had aimed to capture beautiful subject matter, often through slightly soft focus images – was followed by Modernism. Paul Strand's modernist photos 'depict ugly subjects such as a ramshackle suburban corner, telegraph poles, and the close-up of a blind beggar woman, themes with which Strand jolted the onlooker back from the sophisticated dream-world of the aesthetic photographers to the harsh realities of everyday life, which they ignored.'[54] But, paradoxically, such images can spur us to imagine the world differently. As Gesa E. Thiessen has pointed out, reflecting on Picasso's *Guernica* painting: 'Picasso showed his protest against war by confronting the viewer with its horror, thereby pointing to a world that should be other than it is!'[55]

But how can Christians, in good conscience, describe the Cross of Jesus as 'beautiful'? How can his barbaric execution, be anything other than 'ugly'? Especially when words from the book of Isaiah were seen as being fulfilled in the death of Jesus: 'He had no beauty or majesty to attract us to him, nothing in his appearance that we should desire him' (Isaiah 53:2 NIV). Richard Viladesau suggests that we need a 'converted' sense of beauty: 'The cross challenges us to rethink and to expand our notion of the beauty of God, and indeed of "beauty" itself … Physically it was ugly; spiritually – in its meaning, self-sacrifice for others – it was beautiful.'[56]

For Steve, it was the suffering he saw when deployed to places of war with the military that opened his eyes to see the beauty which surrounds us every day. Here we're taking a simple straightforward view of beauty: our working definition is that it is things which make us stop and pause, or, as some might say, that take our breath away. In Christian theology this is called awe and wonder. Steve used to just walk past a flower growing through a crack in a pavement, whereas now he will usually stop and marvel at the intricacy of its shape, and depth of the colours. The psychologist, Richard Tedeschi, has a theory called 'posttraumatic growth'. Within this theory Tedeschi claims trauma can actually enlarge our life and vision, enabling us to see new possibilities in life.[57] Personally, for Steve, those possibilities are seen within the wonder of the life we share with all creation in the world. There is a verse in the Christian Bible which can be translated as: 'We know that all things work together for good for those who love God' (NRSV Romans 8:28). An alternative way of viewing this verse is to see all things as 'intertwining for good'. If we simply say 'things work for good' there is a danger we can see the suffering of war or the illnesses which can limit our life as good. These things are not good in and of themselves, nor wonderful nor beautiful. However, they intertwine within our life experience and, when we recognise this, they can take on a new significance. They do not become good or beautiful, but they form a part of a rich tapestry, of which the whole is beautiful.

The novelist, Umberto Eco, explored the history of beauty.[58] In his book, *On Beauty*, he drew on the historic-aesthetic and artistic understandings of beauty and identified some common factors underlying a sense of beauty. It is a book we would recommend if you are interested in the history of beauty and how it has been defined through different periods. Eco noted how in ancient Greece beauty was seen through the harmony found in various arts. 'Beauty is expressed through the harmony of the cosmos, in poetry it is expressed by the enchantment that makes men [sic] rejoice, in sculpture by the appropriate measure and symmetry of the parts, and in rhetoric by the right rhythm.'[59] Plato developed the idea of beauty and saw it present in both splendour and harmony and proportion between different parts.[60] We often judge things which are well proportioned and sit in symmetry to be beautiful. Looking for the symmetry of things can be a great place to start exploring beauty in our photography. Many artists, photographers and architects recognise the beauty of patterns demonstrating orderliness and following a mathematically described form. Among them, the 'Golden Ratio' and related 'Golden Spiral', both mathematically related to the Fibonacci series of numbers (which goes 0, 1, 1, 2, 3, 5, 8, 13, 21, 34 …), are found in the curve of a snail shell, the human face, the repeating structures within flowers, the position of leaves on trees and even the arms of galaxies, so ubiquitous are these ratios. The Golden Ratio and Golden Spiral are available as overlay guides within most photo apps, to assist in cropping and composing photos in a pleasing way.

However, in Christian terms beauty is about much more than symmetry and harmony. As we have already mentioned, it includes things that evoke awe and wonder – things which make us stop and take our breadth away. We also catch a glimpse of beauty when we see people altruistically giving of themselves to help others – moral beauty. Such beautiful giving need not be limited to us as human beings; consider, for example, the protection an animal affords their young.

The haste of life can make it difficult to glimpse these things and gain a sense of beauty. We often miss what is before us. To see, we have to notice and pay attention to what is there, and this brings us back to the idea of contemplation. Contemplation simply means 'to look at something attentively'. When used in a mindful or contemplative way, a camera helps us slow down and, as we slow down, we see things we might have previously missed through our haste or perhaps because of their sheer ordinariness – things we are so used to seeing that we simply do not notice them anymore. When we slow down and use the camera to help us notice the things of life which surround us, we are seeing afresh and can discover we are surrounded by so much beauty. We discover that beauty is never more than a step away.

To experience beauty is to have your life enlarged, it's about potentially seeing the divine in more and more places, and learning to see how the divine sees. Enzo Bianchi points out that contemplation is about 'the gradual transformation of our gaze so that it becomes like God's way of seeing.'[61] In her book on contemplative photography, Christine Valters Paintner claims: 'when our eyes are graced with wonder, the world reveals its wonders to us.'[62] Put another way, what we see is determined by how we see and when our heart and soul are alive to beauty, we begin to see life in a fresh and energetic way. Jodi Picoult's book, *Small Great Things*, has a scene where a baby is delivered with serious facial deformities and will not live long. The African-American midwife, Ruth, takes this in her stride, but the student nurse who is shadowing her is shocked. Ruth helps the mother, and the father who at first could not look at the child to bond with him in his few hours of life, allowing them to express their love for him. She later says to the student nurse, 'it just goes to show you: every baby is born beautiful. It's what we project on them that makes them ugly'.[63]

The world is a mixture of suffering, of joy, of greed, of self-sacrifice, of justice, of injustice, of ugliness, of wonder and of beauty. Seeing with God's eyes does not seek to deny all the experiences of life which form a part of our journey through life;

and to see with God's eyes opens our eyes to all these things. A part of our attention to life is to notice the beauty that is contained within the ordinary, to be authentic to ourselves and to value all that we are surrounded with.

Exercise 1: Sit comfortably somewhere (inside or outside) and close your eyes. Become aware of your breathing. Do not try to control it but be aware of the feeling of it entering and leaving your body. After a few minutes notice any sounds and sensations, such as people talking or the wind blowing on your face. Don't analysis these, just be aware.

Now open your eyes and observe the space where you are sitting. Notice how the light falls on objects, the placement of things and their interrelationships. Write down one word that summarises what you see. Now go through each of the senses and write one word for each sense. What does it look like, is there a smell, a taste, a sound, a touch? Let your eye rest on one object. Move around it and observe from as many angles as you can. For example, lying down, standing on tiptoe, looking through a gap in the hedge, etc. Having done this, you may want to create some photos from these new perspectives. Are there things you became aware of that you hadn't seen at first when you opened your eyes? What do you feel about the new things you have become aware of? Does the item you are looking at remind you of anything or any situation. Does it act as a metaphor for your life or tell you anything else about your life? Are there things you fail to see because they have become familiar? Are there things that you could try looking at in a new way? Where do you sense beauty in the place you are now standing? Later, in the evening, revisit the pictures you have created. What do you see that is different, where do you see beauty in these images?

Exercise 2: We have noted one ancient aspect of beauty was proportion and order. Go on a walk slowly and purposefully, photographing anything you feel corresponds to this sense of beauty. Later, look at your pictures and notice how you feel, what emotions arise within you? Do these emotions speak into any areas of your own life? Where do you find or fail to find beauty in your life? You may like to discuss your answers with a trusted friend.

Exercise 3: Look at your back catalogue of pictures, printed or on your phone. Thinking about the factors that can give us a sense of beauty, look and see if you can identify them in your pictures. When one picture really grabs you, focus on it, noticing such things as shapes, objects, people, animals, colours, shadows, the fall of light, texture and shape. How is beauty expressed in this picture? Does this picture act as a footprint of your mind revealing the places of beauty in your own life – if so, where are these places? You may like to share your thoughts with a trusted friend.

Exercise 4: Find a picture which you feel is not beautiful. Spend time looking at it and identify the things that mean it is not beautiful. Now ask yourself if the things you have identified speak into any areas of your own life.

Connecting with others – stories secular and sacred

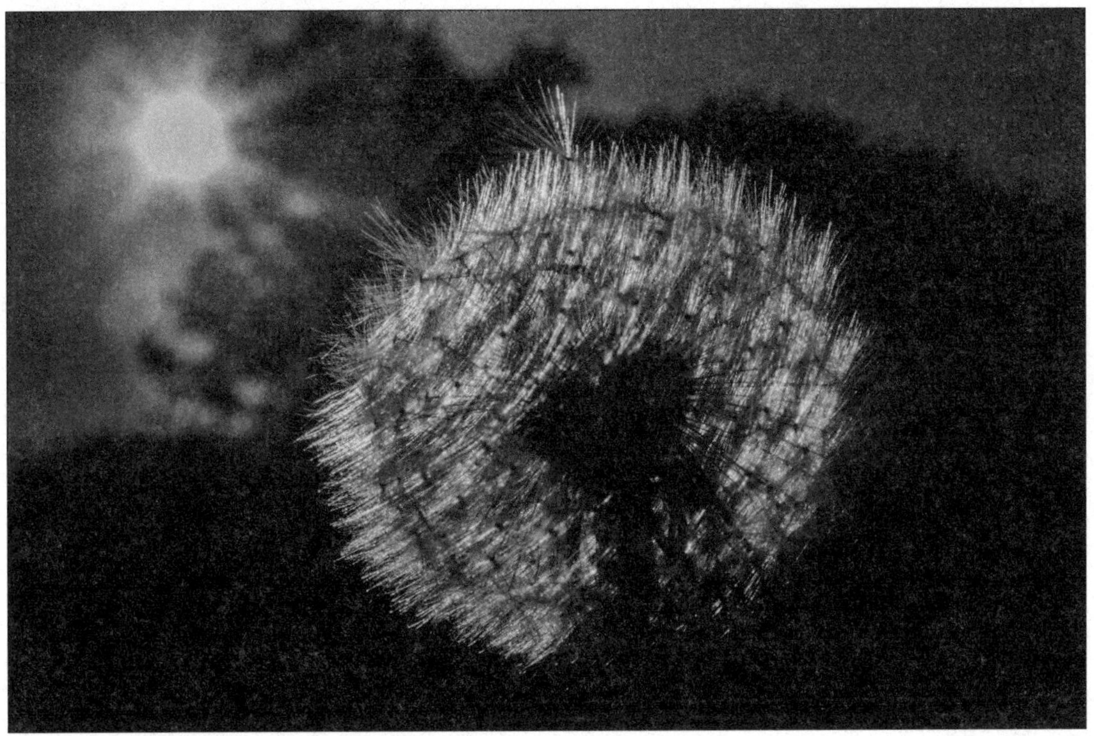

Dandelion Clock © Stephen Radley

Photos can be to us a modern form of parable. Story and parable are closely related, but a parable is told with the intention of igniting interest in a spiritual truth and is generally based on a familiar life experience. Within the Christian tradition the parables that Jesus told are recorded within the Gospels. The parable of the Good Samaritan, where a man has fallen victim to robbers and needs medical help, is popularly assumed to convey the simple truth that anyone in need is our neighbour (Luke 10:25-37). But unlike a preached message, which is direct and limited in meaning, a parable can meet us wherever we are. The power of parable is its ability to speak to each person who hears it in a different way. When people are trained to preach in churches, they are sometimes taught not to explain parables, for to do this reduces their meaning to the linear message of a sermon. Our life experience and choices can make such a linear message exclusive, which shifts us outside the community. A parable allows for multiple interpretations. For example, the parable of the Good Samaritan has many actors within it — a man lying on a road injured and in need of help; a donkey which was to carry the injured man; the robbers; people who walked by and ignored the person who was in need; the inn keeper who provided hospitality; and a Samaritan man who paid for that hospitality, tended the injured man's wounds and used his donkey to carry the man to the inn. On hearing this parable, people often want to be the person who provided the help — he comes across as the hero. Few would want to be the person who has fallen victim to violence, yet this is the place in which we can sometimes find ourselves. We have perhaps all ignored someone who is in need either by literally passing by or preventing their story from being told. When we hear a parable like this it can meet us where we are, because we are invited to see ourselves in the place of one of those actors. At different times in our lives, we will be able to identify with different actors and this is the power of parable — by allowing us to identify with different parts of the story it is not exclusive and invites us to reflect on that identification.

Part of the power of parable is when we share our thoughts with others. This is because other people may see something quite different in the parable, and the same is true for photos. The same photo can evoke quite different emotions, memories and thoughts in each of us. To illustrate what we mean by our claim that photos are a modern form of parable, we will turn to one of Steve's stories:

This section is headed by a picture by Steve of a dandelion. Steve had arrived at a retreat centre in Devon to lead a photography retreat and, as he wandered outside in preparation for the retreat before others arrived, his eye was drawn to a dandelion clock which he spent some time photographing. Talking to a friend later he pondered why in the beauty of the Devonshire countryside he had been drawn to photograph this seemingly dead plant. Reflecting on his life, he had recently left his work and ministry as a chaplain within the RAF, a ministry in which he was experienced, competent and confident, although one which had burnt him out and left him emotionally and spiritually exhausted. Steve said to the person he was sharing the image with, 'this is a bit like my life and ministry, dead and wilted!' His friend, a keen gardener, told him that the dandelion clock is not dead, each seed contains all it needs to sustain life which is why they grow so readily in our lawns. She said, 'it is not dead, simply waiting for the wind to carry it to a new place where it will grow and thrive, bringing life to the bees that drink its nectar and caterpillars that nibble its leaves.'

Reflecting on this picture today, Steve recalls how he had taken several pictures of the dandelions using different directions of light. It was the photograph with the light behind it which really spoke to him at the time and seemed to be telling him without words, to continue towards the light in a new ministry and area of work. It can be easy to keep doing what we have always done, and very often this is the right thing to do, but sometimes our life needs to take a new direction.

We could have placed this story in a reflection about life's choices and patterns, but it sits in this section of our book well as it serves to illustrate how a photo, like a parable, can speak to us and meet us where we are. We mentioned earlier the work of Judy Weiser and how she sees photos as far more than a recording of something we have seen. She suggests that if we notice something we do so because it has some sort of meaning to us. The metaphor she used of 'footprints of the mind' is powerful as it suggests that within a photo we have taken we can potentially see something of our unique mark in the world and how this connects us to one another and to the divine.

Photos can also help us to see one another's worlds, how we each see the world, its threats and its opportunities. We offer a second story to illustrate this idea. Steve had been designing a website with someone, and the site needed to convey a sense of calm. He had used a picture on the home page of his own son silhouetted against a sunset. To Steve this photo held many happy memories of a peaceful time watching the sun set over the sea whilst on holiday. His friend, a young woman, said she felt the picture was oppressive. Confused, Steve asked how a picture which held such memories could be oppressive. His friend explained that what she saw was a lad in a hoodie, and when she walked down dark streets at night men in hoodies sometimes shouted at her which was intimidating. As a man this was something Steve had not personally experienced, but through this photo, and the different way it spoke to his friend, Steve became aware of the intimidation perpetrated by men against women in the way she described. He learned to see the world through his friend's eyes. As we allow photos to speak to us and listen to how they speak to others we can gain greater understanding, and this allows compassion to develop. Fear often thrives when we do not understand the other and we then assume we know their feelings and view of the world. Photos can help us connect with one another through mutual understanding and it is through this that positive change can happen.

Just as a parable can speak to us in different ways, so a photo can speak to us in multiple ways. When we look at a picture alongside another person we can learn to see our own life in a different way and also learn something about the other person that builds our relationship. This connects us to one another and we may also learn to see the connections between our lives and God's story.

Exercise. Our final suggested exercise in this chapter is a simple one and a condensed version of an earlier exercise. With a friend, find a picture together, this can be one you or your friend has taken, one from a magazine, or the Internet. With your friend look at the picture together using a gentle gaze. Take time to look and each notice what memories it evokes and the feelings you feel within you as you gaze at it. Now, in turn share these feelings with each another.

We develop the idea of letting photos speak in groups in our next chapter.

The power of photos to meet us where we are

We have looked at several ways in which photos can speak to us, bringing a greater understanding of self, others, nature and the divine. We have suggested an exercise at the end of each of our reflections with questions you can use to help photos speak to you. Use the questions and exercises that you find helpful. If there are areas which are not helpful to you, then simply ignore and please adapt what we have suggested so it meets your own context better. Photos are a big part of our everyday life, and we hope through this chapter you have gained some ideas on how they can do more than attract 'likes' on our social media or gather dust in an album. We hope you find, like we have, the tremendous power of photos to speak to us and meet us where we are, in an unconditional and non-judgemental way.

CHAPTER 4

Letting photos speak in groups

Why a group?

So far in our book, we've focussed on how photos might be used as a vehicle for personal insight or devotion. There is an additional dimension when we can do this within a small, trusted group. The Bible helps us understand why this may be so, in reflecting on the different gifts with which each human being is blessed. Several passages in the Bible identify lists of God-given gifts (1 Corinthians 12:1-10; Romans 12:6-8; 1 Corinthians 12:28-30; Ephesians 4:11). Although most speak of gifts expressed and offered within the context of a Christian community, there is general agreement that, combined, they enable us to experience and present something of the fullness of Christ. This has been particularly well developed by Alan Hirsch based on the gifts mentioned in Ephesians 4.[64]

The Bible and those interested in spirituality are not alone in classifying human giftings. In more recent years, psychologists have focussed on personality typing. Many organisations use the Myers-Briggs typology to help teams understand how people learn, make decisions, relate and engage with the world and one another. Effective teams, so the theory goes, ideally possess a balance of these personality types.

Christians who have studied the four Myers-Briggs typology pairs (Extrovert-Introvert, Intuitive-Sensing, Thinking-Feeling, Judging-Perceiving) within a spiritual context, argue that they influence preferences and experiences of devotion, prayer, church and even hymnody.[65] Introverts, for example, are energised by individual reflection, whereas Extroverts value the energy of a group discussion. Judgers warm to structured and methodical spiritual techniques, whereas Perceivers seek variety and novelty. When it comes to engaging with an image, Sensors tend to focus on the specific elements present in an image, its colour, shape, the subjects and details revealed and even the feel of the paper on which it is printed. Intuitives, by contrast, often miss the detail, primarily attending to pattern and meaning, drawing on memory and imagination to do so. [66] For them, a photo, and the symbolism within it, is a launchpad for new possibilities ideas and concepts [67]. The wooden drawers in our photo, for example, may evoke ideas of memories acquired over a lifetime, lost and found treasures of experience, and pondering what message the scroll contains. A Sensor, by contrast, may focus on the quality of carpentry, patination and carving of the wood, and fonts used. The Judger will appreciate the orderliness (although probably would want to close the drawers!).

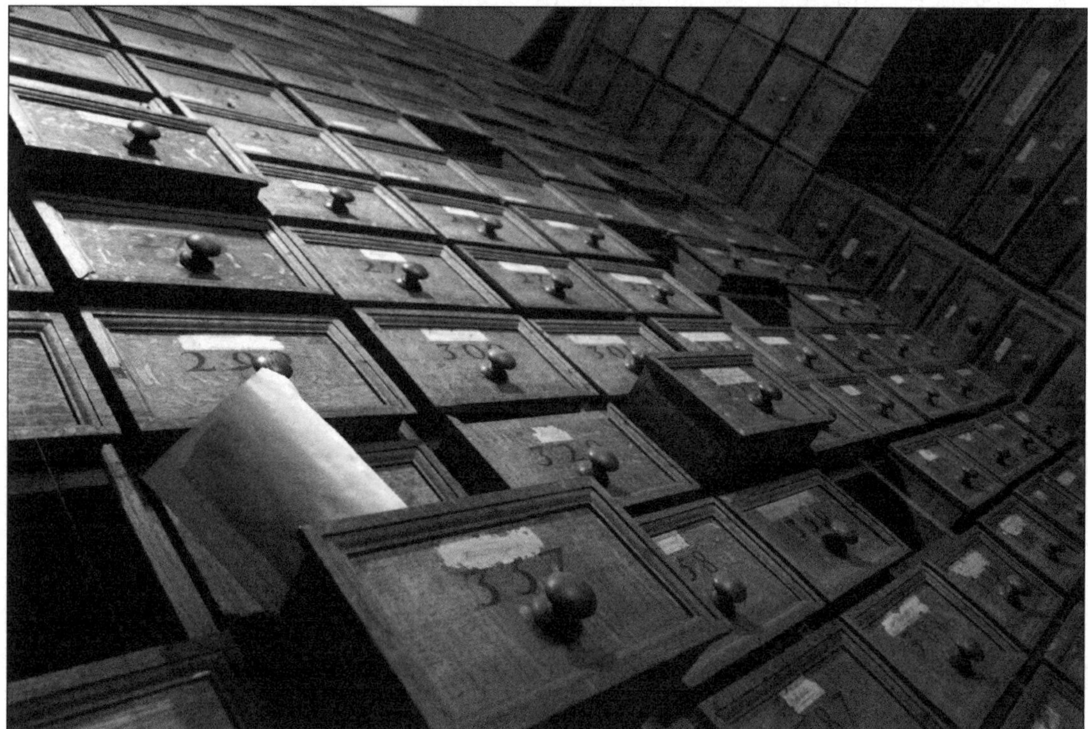

Wooden Drawers © Andy Lindley

Feelers, who tentative statistics suggest are dominant in our church congregations[68] (more so than the population at large[69]), naturally engage with the emotions presented by a photograph. They need no encouragement to place themselves in the shoes of those pictured and imagine both the scene and the feelings it generates. Thinkers being more analytical and word-focussed find this more challenging.

With sixteen combinations of these dipole personality types and a continuous scale between each, you can see what a rich variety of responses there may be to viewing, capturing or interpreting a photo. Jonny Baker would add to this mixture worldviews (or lenses) shaped by 'upbringing, culture, parents, education, class, ethnicity, ways we have been wounded and how we responded to those experiences', which amplify and extend this perceptual variety still further.[70] We would argue that a broad set of perspectives, drawing on as wide a range of different gifts, approaches and viewpoints as possible, will always provide a fuller more balanced and nuanced picture of the world.

These different views and approaches might be compared to the different colours present in the pixels of our TV screens, which combine to give black, white and every hue in between. Myers-Briggs theory encourages us to listen and value the insights of others. Christian spiritual commentators urge us, both individually and as communities, to seek this balance, to both experience the fullness of humanity, but also to fully understand and reflect Jesus, who is our exemplar and, in turn, reflects God. The corollary of this is that, if we seek God's voice, guidance or wisdom through an image or text without this balance present, we risk the distortion of what we discern and instead perceive a God 'made in our image'. This risk is present whether we are interpreting scripture, praying, involved in mission or engaging with our use of photography as a devotional tool.

Having said that, God's Spirit within us can further challenge and expand our narrow viewpoints.[71] A nuance of the Myers-Briggs theory that is of particular value is the notion of our 'shadow'[72] or weaker characteristics. Developing these is obviously a path to wholeness, but, in our experience, pursuing spiritual approaches that engage with our weaker side allows God a chance to be heard above our own 'strong' self. Indeed, simply being open to others for whom our weaknesses are their strength, is to open ourselves more fully to God.

Photos as a third conversation partner

From the beginnings of the Church, Christians have known the value of sharing and building faith within small intimate groups. The opportunity to use photographs to do so is, of course, a much more recent idea and we've reflected in the preceding section why this may be helpful. Cathy Newcomb who leads 'Through the Lens' in South Dakota uses several images to stimulate the core discussion in her worshipping community. Although the whole point of a *visio divina* methodology is that God may speak to you through viewing a photo as an individual, it is within a group that the 'magic happens': Cathy points out, in the 'telling of what made it [*i.e., that photo*] personally meaningful ... This is where you hear God speaking ... and is often more touching and spiritual than any lesson might be'.[73]

Obald Eshleman and Varner Perez are chaplains in a healthcare context. Eshleman describes his photography as a means to 'interact with my inner reality, allowing me to discover, contemplate and express dimensions of my being I intuit but cannot fully express in words'.[74] Eshleman's experience is that some photos, devoid of narrative, have the means to elucidate a profoundly sacred emotional response from those viewing them. In a hospital context, he and Perez describe the images they share with patients, 'as a means of seeing, a medium of sorts: encountering spiritual truths, interpreting their significance, and inviting self-exploration.'[75] Their patients 'saw' themselves projected in the images. One patient, who in his own words didn't do religion, and was initially resistant to conversation, nevertheless revealed, upon viewing an image of a dilapidated shack, that he was a foster kid. The shack became a metaphor of his own broken life, 'with no one home'. The image enabled him to begin to articulate his mental, emotional and physical health, as Eshleman describes, 'providing a back door, into meaning in his life, in which he as chaplain had the privilege of accompanying him'. These feelings, Eshleman and Perez suggest, have sacred qualities, but 'are not outwardly religious; they are about an existential journey into the center (sic.) of one's being, where hidden awareness connects with something greater than oneself.' They summarise their experience with patients, by describing the photos as acting as a 'third thing' or a 'third voice' in their conversations.[76] Extending this still further, and recognising the sacred quality of these experiences, they describe the images as 'interceding between the chaplain and patient, creating an experiential dynamic'.[77] We might even allow, through the Holy Spirit, that the images become vehicles for a divine voice and presence. However, we are not sure every photo has the richness, depth and creative presence to achieve this high bar, and even the 'right' photos, Eshleman reminds us, require a receptivity and emotional and spiritual openness from those present to do so.

Nevertheless, our experience is that photos still have value in less emotionally charged or challenging environments. Divine Focus, which we will explore in more detail shortly, is a church drawing on photography and utilising images within worship, led by Andy. When it first met, they used an array of around 100 photos, laid upon the altar table and pre-selected to engage with different personality types, as a means to respond to what the group had previously shared and to move into a time of prayer. This placement deliberately drew on the symbolism of offering, divine encounter and communion, which the table normally facilitated. This visual 'toolkit', used each week, comprised a selection of their own photos, cuttings from National Geographic magazines and some from photo sites like Pixabay.com. [78]

At the conclusion of the time of worship, they invited each person to select a photo from the selection that 'spoke' to them and to then spend a few moments in silence, praying with it. Each person was then encouraged to offer a sentence or two of prayer or share briefly how the photo has spoken to them. For many people, there is a significant reticence to speaking in a group context and, even more so, to share vulnerably and openly in an unrehearsed way. Somehow, however, that same experiential dynamic of the 'third voice', or 'conversation partner', is present even in the simple selection of a photo. Inherently, the act of showing their photo to the group reveals something of their internal dialogue and begins to break down the barriers they may have erected. Even for those more confident in public reflecting, it was noticeable that their sharing was often deeper, personally revelatory, or more intimate than initially intended. This depth of sharing echoes the sacred 'magic' Cathy Newcomb describes at 'Through the Lens' and enriches the experience for everyone concerned. Wonderfully, unlike lots of worship practices, this works for all ages.

A practical example: Divine Focus

'Divine Focus' is a worship gathering that centres on images and photography, led by Andy since 2019, which draws on many of the techniques and practices we've so far explored.[79]

The theme, together with an associated piece of scripture, is provided at least a month in advance of the meeting. Those gathering are encouraged to submit up to six photos, a few days in advance of the meeting, and to be prepared to share their thoughts and reflections during our communal worship. This number of images allows for a theme to be unpacked and ideas developed, but needs to be balanced by the time available for each person to share so the overall time of worship is not too extended.

The process of selecting and reflecting on photos, individually, is then broadly similar to that of 'Discovery' and theological reflection outlined in Chapter 2, with the exception that each image, as acquired and engaged with, becomes a new conversation partner in that process. Andy's biblical tutors at college demonstrated how we might use the Bible to interpret itself, with different verses juxtaposed leading to deeper understanding, Similarly, each photograph interprets, explores and expands upon both the theme and the other photos. This is illustrated in a simple way, within this trio of photos, presented in response to the theme of 'Spirit Fire' and verses from Acts 2:1-4, which describe the Spirit descending as tongues of fire on the disciples of Jesus. The photos help us reflect on this metaphor for Spirit, by contrasting fire – as servant to human industry, creativity and fun – with its destructive and unpredictable nature.

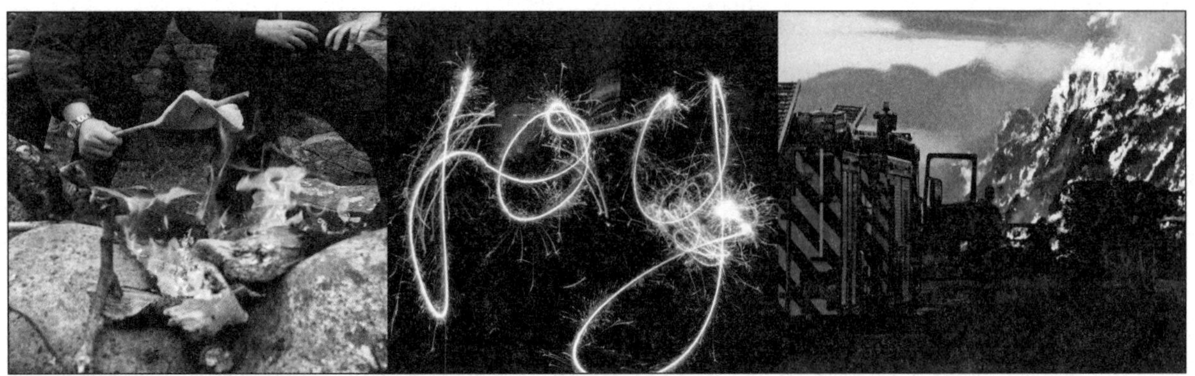

Joy © Andy Lindley

Allowing the image selection process to take place over a number of weeks, one finds oneself in a spiritual dialogue and ongoing conversation with God in everyday life. This may be a new paradigm for those whose relationship with God is focused on specific moments set aside for devotions. Indeed, it may awaken us to other sources of God's voice, within the music we listen to, television we watch, the people we meet, conversations we hold and the other scriptures and literary materials we are reading.

We hope, in our sharing so far, we've inspired you that using a camera and capturing photos can be in itself a spiritual exercise. However, there are practical and pragmatic reasons why sometimes this is not an option.

A viable alternative, if you have been a prolific photographer, is to turn to your back catalogues. Whether they be print or digital archives, there is joy in revisiting old photo collections. Memories of treasured events, holidays, family photos, and people long-cherished but now passed away, can be triggered. For those of us who have long used our cameras with a spiritual focus, it is a way of revisiting the meanings and the thoughts associated with some of the photos we've previously reflected on, or which have spoken to us as we captured them. Akin to a spiritual journaling process,[80] it is an opportunity to revisit these reflections.

We've recently discovered that, if your photo collection is largely digital, with the help of appropriate software, elements of the photos can be recognised and catalogued by AI (Artificial Intelligence) processes. Images stored in either Google or Amazon drives can undergo a degree of automatic cataloguing, potentially recognising landmarks as well as places and people. An intriguing exercise, while viewing your online albums, is to type into the search engine some keywords around the theme and see what the AI offers you. Like our Sensor gifted friends (see above), the AIs are better at labelling objects than feelings or symbols. Nevertheless, occasionally they will offer up some photos that surprise you. Often this has led us to explore the nominated Divine Focus theme from a new viewpoint.

The final unexpected advantage of having your photos stored in the 'Cloud'[81] is that if you also have a device or smart TV and use Amazon Prime or Google Chrome, then you can set your TV screensaver to draw on your photo collection. Just occasionally, a photo has 'found us' through appearing on the screen at an opportune moment, and spoken into something we have been wrestling with, or praying about. God moves in mysterious ways!

The Divine Focus Gathering

Having collated our photos, with a means to present them, our worship gatherings then have a simple shape:

- reviewing and exploring the theme;
- sharing our photos: individual and collective responses;
- drawing together the threads;
- a responsive time of prayer.

After briefly reviewing our theme and reading the associated scripture, we first briefly re-examine the context of our selected verses within the wider biblical narrative or draw on other verses of scripture that shed further light on the theme. Occasionally we draw on a technique espoused by Jonny Baker,[82] which is reminiscent of an Ignatian approach whereby we use our senses to imagine ourselves within a Bible story, but doing so as if we were a photographer on the scene, seeking to capture a single image that will illustrate the key message or events.

The aim of engaging with the theme, using biblical interpretation, is that we begin to alter the lens, as it were, with which we will review our photos. The next stage is simple, each person individually presents their set of photos, and shares their reflections. In a small gathering, we allow 5-6 minutes per person. In a larger gathering, it may be helpful either to limit the number of photos or break into smaller groups. As with a workshop (see below), this is not a time for others to critique or judge the quality of photos, but rather it is an opportunity to hear an individual 'third voice' dialogue with each photo as 'conversation partner', as well as listening to the individual's own reflections. Occasionally, if the photos stir something for another person or they reveal something unseen by those presenting it, we may share together briefly, but largely that sharing is saved for a time of collective response after all the photos are presented. The primary goal of the collective response period is that through opening ourselves to the reflections of others, filtered through their own diverse theological reflections, worldviews, personalities and life experiences, we might hear more fully God's voice.

When all the photos have been shared, we draw together the threads of our reflections and try to discern and distil how God has spoken to us, as a worshipping community and, just as importantly, as individuals, through our diverse viewpoints. These thoughts we take into our final responsive prayers.

Workshops

Workshops are another group context into which photos can speak. A workshop combining spirituality and photography typically brings together a group of people who may or may not previously know each other, often in a particularly photogenic location. It will include input from the leader, for instance, expanding on some of the themes in the book, *Spirituality in Photography*,[83] or introducing exercises for cultivating a more receptive and less 'one-track' gaze. Crucially, it will also involve hands-on experience out and about with one's camera or smartphone. Participants may simply be invited to explore the area with their cameras or, alternatively, they might try out some of the ideas suggested by the workshop input, for example, to do with 'slower photography', use of perspective or framing. Or there may be a set theme for the day, such as 'the fruits of the Spirit'. A church may choose to explore its vision for the future through a photo workshop and ask participants to make pictures showing, say, the story of their local church and community.

Not everyone finds it easy to create images on a particular theme, so, inevitably, some themes will be less collectively relevant. Themes also sometimes need in practice to be adapted. For instance, 'Winter meets its Death'[84] was going to be the theme of a workshop held in South-East England in late March 2018, inviting participants to explore the coming of Spring and burgeoning new life. In the event, it was an unseasonable bitterly cold day, after heavy snowfall, and so raw that no one could venture outside for more than a few minutes. Photography took place inside the workshop venue instead — a beautiful rural parish church.

It is important that participants get the chance to share the photos they have been making later at the workshop. Some may come back early from their photo exploration to get one-to-one technical guidance from the workshop leader about using their camera to full effect. But everyone should be encouraged, though not pressurised, to share some of their photos with the whole group. The challenge, however, is how. The most basic way is to display photos on your camera or smartphone's LED screen and carefully pass this around the group. Ideally, however, the images should be projected or printed, from copies emailed or transferred via a memory card. Achieving this may take some time and technical skill. If it's not feasible to have a laptop, video projector and/or inkjet printer available at the workshop, it might be worth investing, instead, in a handheld smartphone printer to produce small prints to pass around.

When a photo is shared at a workshop, feedback is invited from the group, with a clear understanding that comments should be about the meaning(s) of the image and not its technical merits or demerits. A useful starting technique is to go around the group and ask each person to say a single word about the image and then ask the photographer to say what drew them to make the image and how it speaks to them. This helps to prevent any one person dominating the discussion and also appeals to the more diffident and reticent, who are only initially being asked to contribute one word. In our experience, this technique has extraordinary power to release individuals who generally feel inarticulate or ignored to share their responses to photos. If appropriate, this can be followed by once again going around the group, this time inviting all participants to share a brief sentence or experience inspired by the photo, if they wish. It's important that no one feels pressed to participate, but also that they appreciate there are no 'right' or 'wrong' comments and that each person's perspective is valued.

Letting a photo speak and receiving group comments can have significant personal impact for the photographer. For instance, an image was taken by one workshop participant of a woodland scene leading to a gate. One of those subsequently viewing the image was curious as to what lay beyond the gate and the photographer explained that they didn't know as they had not ventured that far. At this point another participant mentioned that they had gone up to the gate and had realised that the ground dropped away steeply on the other side – hence one couldn't see beyond the gate in the photo. Feedback received later from the photographer revealed that taking the photo and the group reflection had helped them realise that they were facing a difficult life decision and tending to shy away from it. The photo helped them clarify what they needed to do.

Using photos in more traditional worship

Although in our book we hope to have already encouraged the use of photos as a personal and group devotional or insight tool, we recognise that in many churches today images have also had something of a renaissance. Historically conveyed through murals, paintings, floral decoration and stained glass and once largely expunged under Protestant puritanical fervour, they have made a reappearance, utilising the now ubiquitous video-projector and coloured wash-lighting, for instance. The images used, however, often still echo those ancient practices, such as glorifying God through decorative beauty. The colourful light, once played through stained glass windows and painting the church interior with light, may be replaced by ever-renewable images projected on a screen or, more imaginatively, such as in York Minster's annual light celebration, once again upon the fabric of the building itself. Stained glass images were also a primary story-telling medium for a largely illiterate population. Projected images and modern artworks continue to be used to illustrate and interpret public reading of the scriptures, stories or talks, in a similar way. A further nuance to this is that the projected image might convey a secondary narrative alongside the spoken word. This might be one that explores a specific context for the expressed ideas, but is also useful in speaking to those with different learning preferences, sensory limitations, or simply sharing age-differentiated needs. Similarly, images can either offer a summary of a complex idea or provoke a more in-depth reflection of a relatively simple idea. They can act as both a memory jogger and be a simple takeaway for those who process more readily after the fact.

Tradition dictates that there is a fairly standard rhythm, flow and pattern to worship; and, for those that value this approach, regularly-used liturgies and forms of words can shortcut those worshipping into the different spiritual modes of adoration, confession, listening, responding, intercessory prayer, and suchlike. We have found that regularly-used images can offer a visual liturgy that similarly aids the worshipper. Designed well, the images themselves, without explanation, can evoke a suitable emotion or mood, making worship for those new to it more accessible. A peaceful, beautiful pastoral scene, for example, evokes calm, while a bustling, dynamic, energetic image encourages response and action. An image of people holding hands might lend a communal aspect to an intercessional responsive prayer. Likewise, images can help frame worship. We usually offer an image at the start of worship, that we then return to throughout, that acts as: i) preparation, evoking curiosity and beginning the process of engaging with the worship; ii) companion to the sermon or discussion, where we perhaps draw out ideas that might be present in the image; and iii) reminder, as a final image to remind us of the journey we have shared. 'Tell 'em what you are going to tell 'em; tell 'em; tell 'em what you told 'em', as the saying goes. Alternatively, we may transform the original image itself, as we unpack an idea, thereby offering a visual narrative, alongside the spoken one.

Often we can use images to challenge a superficial interpretation of ideas and concepts, rather than merely to illustrate the ideas in a passage of scripture or hymn. For example, the carol 'Silent Night' may have more challenge and power when coupled with an image of English and German soldiers leaving their trenches to play football at Christmas in 1914. Such a juxtaposition invites a reflection on the tension between promise and reality at Christmas, and yet continues to include the eschatological hope present in Jesus' birth. Similarly, creative cognitive dissonance can be achieved by displaying images of poverty, alongside scripture or songs speaking of God's abundant blessing. Finally, and most particularly when it comes to interpreting scripture or seeking to evoke a practical response, we can contextualise a general idea, such as helping the poor, with a local image of, say, a food bank in our neighbourhood, offering a concrete example as to how one might respond.

Reflecting on all that, it is far from surprising that the historical attempt to suppress images in worship did not just fail, but perhaps led to an explosion of creative new uses, which, as they were once intended, enable more people to access worship in ways fruitful for their own spiritual needs.

CHAPTER 5

Building a personal photo journal — a modern 'Book of Hours'

The final chapter of this book offers some templates for you to build your own personal photo journal. We invite you to add some of your most personally-significant photos to the closing pages of the book and write about the meanings these images hold for you. Using some of the ideas explored earlier in this book, we encourage you to let your photos speak. There will be options simply to explore your pictures in secular terms or to dig deeper spiritually.

We will also provide extra copies of the templates online, so that you can create additional personal photo journals. You could, if you wish, simply complete and store your photo journals on your computer, but we encourage you to create hard copies with your own handwritten reflections. Printed photos are material objects, appealing not just to our sense of sight but also to our sense of touch (and potentially even the sense of smell). We can handle them, look at them in different lighting conditions and revisit them year on year. By contrast, photos viewed on a computer or device screen are backlit and remote and potentially ephemeral if you have a hardware failure. Handwriting your accompanying reflections is much more personal than hitting a keyboard. If and when in the future you look back at your reflections you may be able to identify with the words more fully, written as they are in your own hand. Alternatively, of course, your thinking may have changed and you may hardly believe that these were your words then, but your handwriting proves the case!

A hard copy personal photo journal is something tangible that you can carry with you or keep somewhere safe, to revisit whenever you like. It is something that you can choose to keep completely private to yourself or you may decide to show it to other people such as a particular 'soul friend' or a spiritual director.

You may wish to write some prayers in your photo journal alongside the images. Our templates will offer you a simple way of creating a prayer out of your reflections. Perhaps your photo journal will then begin to resemble somewhat a medieval 'Book of Hours'. Immensely popular amongst wealthy laypeople, a Book of Hours was a personalised prayer book punctuated with colourful, richly-decorated images of incidents from the Bible and the lives of saints. Sometimes the pictures were crafted by leading artists, such as the great Renaissance illustrator, Simon Bening (see Image 10). Purchasers could individually choose which images and prayers would be included in their Book of Hours.

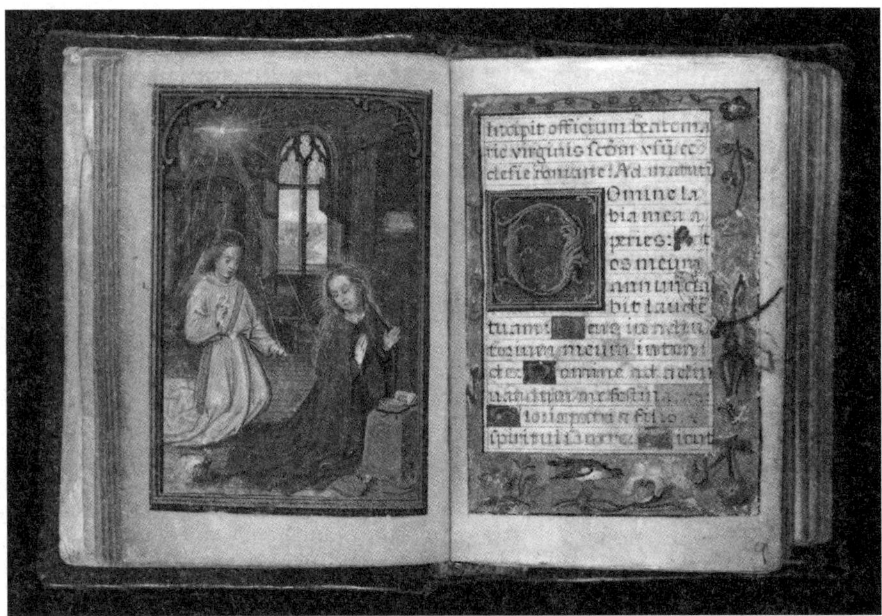

Book of Hours, Simon Bening (Netherlandish) ca. 1530–35, Metropolitan Museum of Art, accession number 2015.706 (Public Domain)

They were called books of hours because they were designed to be aids to devotion and focuses for meditation at regular points every day. This meant that laypeople could emulate the devotions of monks and nuns, who would say the Divine Office together at eight set times during the day and night (although laypeople were not necessarily expected to engage in the night time devotions and might leave them till they got up!). A key element in every Book of Hours was the 'Hours of the Virgin', a series of prayers and praise centred on the Virgin Mary, intended to be said at the eight set points each day. There were also additional elements that purchasers could choose to include, such as a calendar of feast days, Gospel lessons, prayers to the saints, penitential psalms, or 'Hours of the Cross' focussing on the Passion and Crucifixion of Jesus.

The paintings in books of hours were not simply illustrations to conveniently divide up the book or make it look more attractive. They were intended to be used for meditation and have been called 'painted prayers'.[85] The number of pictures included in books of hours varied according to what the owner could afford. The more expensive books of hours would include a picture of a different aspect of the Christmas story at the beginning of each of the eight 'Hours of the Virgin'. Later books of hours began to be printed in bulk, but the earliest were handmade, with pictures individually crafted to the buyer's own specification. Books of hours were a much-treasured resource for contemplation and devotion. Perhaps your personal photo journal might become a modern reinvention of a Book of Hours as you combine your images with your reflections and maybe prayers?

We invite you, when you're ready, to begin using the five templates we have provided to produce your own personal photo journal. We have prefaced the templates with a worked example of how *visio divina* might be applied to a photo. There is also a worked example of how someone might 'dig deeper' if they were a person of faith. This is just an example of how one person used the template. You may choose to respond to the prompts in the templates in quite different ways.

The starting point always will be one of your photos that stands out for you and invites your attention. It will be important to allow yourself plenty of time to reacquaint yourself with your photo and maybe begin to notice things you hadn't seen before. Because you were the photographer, you will also have the opportunity to trawl your memory of why you took the photo and the meanings it had for you originally. We suggest you don't begin to fill in the template until you have spent an unhurried time contemplating your photo. It may take much longer than you expect to fill in the template, as you carefully reflect on the questions posed. Remember, there are no right or wrong answers and you can choose to keep what you write for your eyes only.

Once you have completed reflecting on your photo and filling in the template, you will have something that you can look back on as a record of what the photo has meant to you. We have supplied you with an overlay bookmark that will automatically transform what you have written into a narrative. You just need to lay the bookmark on the left-hand side of the relevant page. When it comes to the 'Digging Deeper' template, the associated bookmark will not only create a narrative of what you have written, but will, if you turn it over, produce a simple prayer based on what you have written. Of course, if you are already experienced at creating prayers you may instead decide to write your own prayer from scratch.

EXAMPLE TEMPLATE

The next four pages provide an example
by Philip Richter of
how the templates can be used.

LETTING MY PHOTO SPEAK	TITLE OF PHOTO [write in box on right]	*Time stands still — Saint Pierre Basilica, Avignon*
What draws your eye in this photo?	**My eye is drawn by …** [write in box on right]	*the little lane running off to the right and the door in the church wall with a pointed arch; I then look across to the cycle leaning against the church railings*
What triggered you taking this photo?	**I was first triggered into taking this photo by …** [write in box on right]	*wanting to photograph details of the church exterior, rather than the whole magnificent Gothic façade, whilst also wanting to exclude other tourists from the scene; it was then that I noticed the mysterious and rather narrow lane leading out of the picture and waited till it was empty of people before pressing the shutter*
How does this photo make you feel?	**I feel …** [write in box on right]	*nostalgia for happy days spent in Avignon, as well as a sense of curiosity about what might be round the corner along the lane; also a creative tension between ancient and new: the photo might have been taken much earlier in the church's history, were it not for the modern cycle, bundle of electrical wiring and CCTV camera*
How might this picture help you make sense of a situation in your life, or the world at the moment?	**It could help me make sense of …** [write in box on right]	*retirement, downsizing and moving to a new home: there is an implicit invitation in the picture to explore a new future whilst not tearing up the past; the cycle seems to symbolise movement: albeit diminutive compared to the heights of history in the architecture behind it, the cycle is not intended to remain chained to the railings but might take one in an altogether unexpected direction*

What one word comes to mind when you look at this photo?	**The one word that comes to mind is …** [write in box on right]	*turning*
Any important event in your life that it reminds you of?	**It reminds me of when …** [write in box on right]	*I spent time in another ancient French city during a sabbatical, when I was researching a photo essay about how different parts of Europe celebrated Sunday and discovered that, at least then, Sunday in France was a much valued and distinctive day of rest, restoring people for the week ahead. When remembering this, I appreciated the need to slow down and rest before taking new directions.*
Any important person in your life that it reminds you of?	**It reminds me of …** [write in box on right]	*David, a friend who fearlessly rides his bike through congested streets, occasionally falls off and injures himself, and radiates a keen sense of spiritual equilibrium, balancing work and play, personal and outward-facing religion, light-heartedness and gravity. When remembering this, I appreciated the need to cultivate a sense of balance in my own life.*
What might this photo be telling you about yourself?	**That I …** [write in box on right]	*need to have an expansive gaze in my life — looking to the past, the present and the future, attending to the finer details as well as the big picture; and that I need times of stillness and reflection as well as frenetic activity*
Does this bring to mind, a story, a song, or a poem?	**It brings to mind …** [write in box on right]	*the poem, 'The Road Not Taken' by Robert Frost (in Mountain Interval, New York: Henry Holt and Co, 1916) with its closing lines: 'Two roads diverged in a wood, and I — I took the one less traveled by, And that has made all the difference.' It's a complex poem, but currently I'm seeing it as a challenge to move forward in a direction I have so far less travelled.*

DIGGING DEEPER **Anything about God that it reminds you of?**	**It reminds me that God …** [write in box on right]	*is a God of reliance and stability, but also of mystery and wonder*
What might this photo be telling you about yourself, in the light of your faith?	**That I …** [write in box on right]	*need to connect myself fully to the present moment and also be ready to explore new pathways; as well as keeping in touch with the past and all that has made me who I am*
What might God be saying to you through your photo? God is saying …	**God is saying …** [write in box on right]	*I am the God of yesterday, today and tomorrow, ever-old and ever-new*
Is there anything you'd like to say to God now after reflecting on your photo?	**I'd say …** [write in box on right]	*let me not be afraid to turn new corners and find the rich surprises you are waiting to share with me*
Anything you most want to do/be as a result of reflecting on your photo?	**I'd like to…** [write in box on right]	*be more trusting for the future*
(purposely left blank)		
Any other insights that you have received, thanks to pausing with this photo?	**And there were other insights too, thanks to having paused with this photo …**	Other insights — *I remembered that I had taken this photo on a holiday celebrating my retirement from full-time work, at an important time of transition and change in my life. I see the photo as a gift from God to help me explore new beginnings*

MY PHOTO

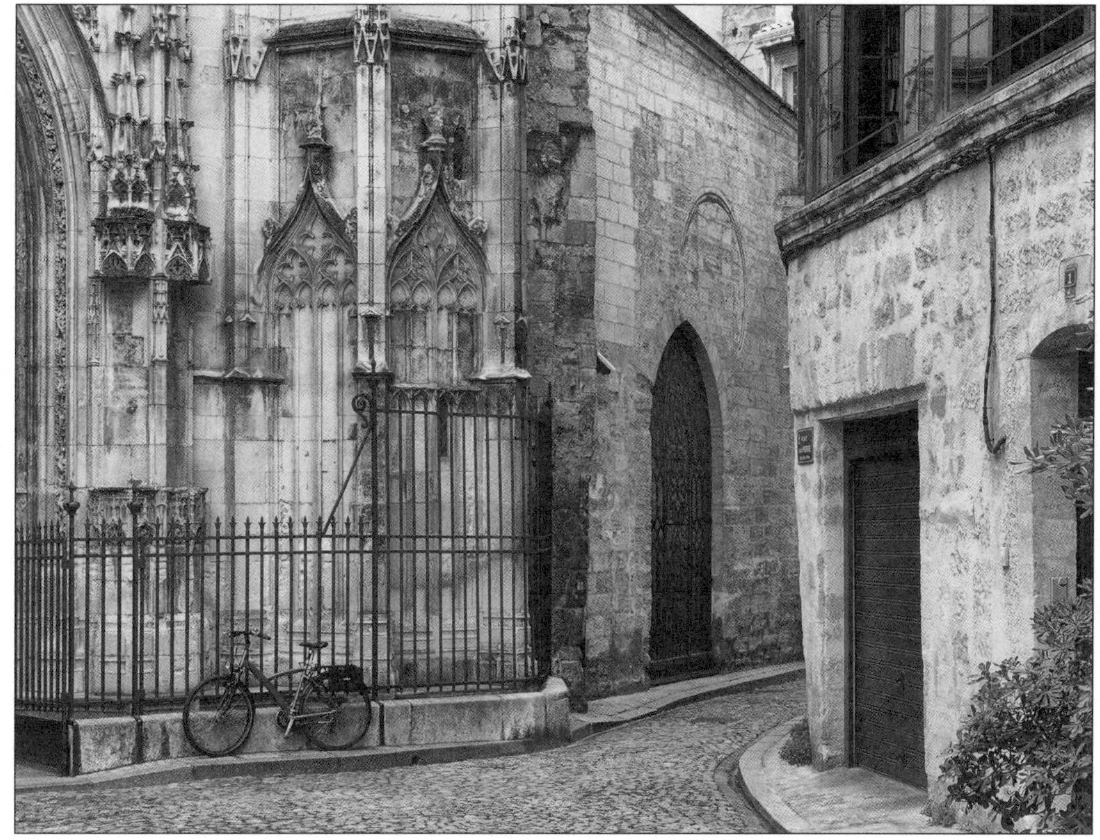

Time stands still — St Pierre Basilica, Avignon © Philip Richter

TEMPLATES

The following pages provide
templates for you to use.
Further copies are available at
http://www.soulfulvision.uk/lps

LETTING MY PHOTO SPEAK	**TITLE OF PHOTO** [write in box on right]	
What draws your eye in this photo?	**My eye is drawn by …** [write in box on right]	
What triggered you taking this photo?	**I was first triggered into taking this photo by …** [write in box on right]	
How does this photo make you feel?	**I feel …** [write in box on right]	
How might this picture help you make sense of a situation in your life, or the world at the moment?	**It could help me make sense of …** [write in box on right]	

What one word comes to mind when you look at this photo?	**The one word that comes to mind is…** [write i n box on right]	
Any important event in your life that it re-minds you of?	**It reminds me of when …** [write in box on right]	
Any important person in your life that it re-minds you of?	**It reminds me of …** [write in box on right]	
What might this photo be telling you about yourself?	**That I …** [write in box on right]	
Does this bring to mind, a story, a song, or a poem?	**It brings to mind …** [write in box on right]	

DIGGING DEEPER Anything about God that it reminds you of?	**It reminds me that God ...** [write in box on right]	
What might this photo be telling you about yourself, in the light of your faith?	**That I ...** [write in box on right]	
What might God be saying to you through your photo? God is saying ...	**God is saying ...** [write in box on right]	
Is there anything you'd like to say to God now after reflecting on your photo?	**I'd say ...** [write in box on right]	
Anything you most want to do/be as a result of reflecting on your photo?	**I'd like to ...** [write in box on right]	
(purposely left blank)		
Any other insights that you have received, thanks to pausing with this photo?	**And there were other insights too, thanks to having paused with this photo ...**	

MY PHOTO

LETTING MY PHOTO SPEAK	TITLE OF PHOTO [write in box on right]	
What draws your eye in this photo?	My eye is drawn by … [write in box on right]	
What triggered you taking this photo?	I was first triggered into taking this photo by … [write in box on right]	
How does this photo make you feel?	I feel … [write in box on right]	
How might this picture help you make sense of a situation in your life, or the world at the moment?	It could help me make sense of … [write in box on right]	

What one word comes to mind when you look at this photo?	**The one word that comes to mind is …** [write in box on right]	
Any important event in your life that it reminds you of?	**It reminds me of when …** [write in box on right]	
Any important person in your life that it reminds you of?	**It reminds me of …** [write in box on right]	
What might this photo be telling you about yourself?	**That I …** [write in box on right]	
Does this bring to mind, a story, a song, or a poem?	**It brings to mind …** [write in box on right]	

DIGGING DEEPER Anything about God that it reminds you of?	**It reminds me that God …** [write in box on right]	
What might this photo be telling you about yourself, in the light of your faith?	**That I …** [write in box on right]	
What might God be saying to you through your photo? God is saying …	**God is saying …** [write in box on right]	
Is there anything you'd like to say to God now after reflecting on your photo?	**I'd say …** [write in box on right]	
Anything you most want to do/be as a result of re-flecting on your photo?	**I'd like to …** [write in box on right]	
(purposely left blank)		
Any other insights that you have received, thanks to pausing with this photo?	**And there were other insights too, thanks to having paused with this photo …**	

MY PHOTO

LETTING MY PHOTO SPEAK	TITLE OF PHOTO [write in box on right]	
What draws your eye in this photo?	**My eye is drawn by …** [write in box on right]	
What triggered you taking this photo?	**I was first triggered into taking this photo by …** [write in box on right]	
How does this photo make you feel?	**I feel …** [write in box on right]	
How might this picture help you make sense of a situation in your life, or the world at the moment?	**It could help me make sense of …** [write in box on right]	

What one word comes to mind when you look at this photo?	**The one word that comes to mind is …** [write in box on right]	
Any important event in your life that it reminds you of?	**It reminds me of when …** [write in box on right]	
Any important person in your life that it reminds you of?	**It reminds me of …** [write in box on right]	
What might this photo be telling you about yourself?	**That I …** [write in box on right]	
Does this bring to mind, a story, a song, or a poem?	**It brings to mind …** [write in box on right]	

DIGGING DEEPER Anything about God that it reminds you of?	**It reminds me that God ...** [write in box on right]	
What might this photo be telling you about yourself, in the light of your faith?	**That I ...** [write in box on right]	
What might God be saying to you through your photo? God is saying ...	**God is saying ...** [write in box on right]	
Is there anything you'd like to say to God now after reflecting on your photo?	**I'd say ...** [write in box on right]	
Anything you most want to do/be as a result of reflecting on your photo?	**I'd like to ...** [write in box on right]	
(purposely left blank)		
Any other insights that you have received, thanks to pausing with this photo?	**And there were other insights too, thanks to having paused with this photo ...**	

MY PHOTO

LETTING MY PHOTO SPEAK	TITLE OF PHOTO [write in box on right]	
What draws your eye in this photo?	**My eye is drawn by ...** [write in box on right]	
What triggered you taking this photo?	**I was first triggered into taking this photo by ...** [write in box on right]	
How does this photo make you feel?	**I feel ...** [write in box on right]	
How might this picture help you make sense of a situation in your life, or the world at the moment?	**It could help me make sense of ...** [write in box on right]	

What one word comes to mind when you look at this photo?	The one word that comes to mind is ... [write in box on right]	
Any important event in your life that it reminds you of?	It reminds me of when ... [write in box on right]	
Any important person in your life that it reminds you of?	It reminds me of ... [write in box on right]	
What might this photo be telling you about yourself?	That I ... [write in box on right]	
Does this bring to mind, a story, a song, or a poem?	It brings to mind ... [write in box on right]	

DIGGING DEEPER Anything about God that it reminds you of?	**It reminds me that God …** [write in box on right]	
What might this photo be telling you about yourself, in the light of your faith?	**That I …** [write in box on right]	
What might God be saying to you through your photo? God is saying …	**God is saying …** [write in box on right]	
Is there anything you'd like to say to God now after reflecting on your photo?	**I'd say …** [write in box on right]	
Anything you most want to do/be as a result of re-flecting on your photo?	**I'd like to …** [write in box on right]	
(purposely left blank)		
Any other insights that you have received, thanks to pausing with this photo?	**And there were other insights too, thanks to having paused with this photo …**	

MY PHOTO

LETTING MY PHOTO SPEAK	**TITLE OF PHOTO** [write in box on right]	
What draws your eye in this photo?	**My eye is drawn by …** [write in box on right]	
What triggered you taking this photo?	**I was first triggered into taking this photo by …** [write in box on right]	
How does this photo make you feel?	**I feel …** [write in box on right]	
How might this picture help you make sense of a situation in your life, or the world at the moment?	**It could help me make sense of …** [write in box on right]	

What one word comes to mind when you look at this photo?	The one word that comes to mind is ... [write in box on right]	
Any important event in your life that it reminds you of?	It reminds me of when ... [write in box on right]	
Any important person in your life that it reminds you of?	It reminds me of ... [write in box on right]	
What might this photo be telling you about yourself?	That I ... [write in box on right]	
Does this bring to mind, a story, a song, or a poem?	It brings to mind ... [write in box on right]	

DIGGING DEEPER Anything about God that it reminds you of?	**It reminds me that God …** [write in box on right]	
What might this photo be telling you about yourself, in the light of your faith?	**That I …** [write in box on right]	
What might God be saying to you through your photo? God is saying …	**God is saying …** [write in box on right]	
Is there anything you'd like to say to God now after reflecting on your photo?	**I'd say …** [write in box on right]	
Anything you most want to do/be as a result of reflecting on your photo?	**I'd like to …** [write in box on right]	
(purposely left blank)		
Any other insights that you have received, thanks to pausing with this photo?	**And there were other insights too, thanks to having paused with this photo …**	

MY PHOTO

BOOKMARK OVERLAYS

The next two pages contain bookmarks
for you to cut out and lay over the
templates to provide a reflective
narrative on your photograph.

TITLE OF PHOTO	If I had to sum up the photo in one word, it would be …	
When I spent time looking at this photo my eye was especially drawn by…	**The photo stirred up some significant memories for me. It reminded me of an important event in my life when…**	to make double-sided bookmark: cut out and fold in half vertically ←
I was first triggered into taking this photo by…	**It also reminded me of someone important in my life…**	
The photo made me feel…	**I found the photo was telling me that I …**	
I felt the photo had the potential to help me make sense of a situation that was troubling me:	**The photo had special resonance for me: it brought to mind …**	

NARRATIVE	PRAYER	DIGGING DEEPER
The photo reminded me that God	Loving God, who …	to make double-sided bookmark: cut out and fold in half vertically ←
I found the photo was telling me that I …	Thank you for the gift of this photo. Thank you for helping me discover more about myself through this photo, that I …	
I got the sense that God was speaking to me somehow through the photo and saying …	Help me, through this photo, to hear you saying to me:	
In response, I wanted to say to God that …	Lord, …	
After reflecting on the photo, I particularly wanted to …	Fill me your grace and mercy and help me to …	
	For I ask this in the name of Jesus. Amen.	
And there were other insights too, thanks to having paused with this photo …	Why not make the prayer your own by praying it?	

Over to you...

In this book, we have shared parts of our own journeys and how photography has helped us as authors explore and feel connected to the world, the divine, nature and others. We have each found in our different ways that photography can have beneficial effects on our wellbeing through the interconnections between contemplation and mindfulness. We have outlined some ways of exploring meanings in photos, ranging from theological reflection to *visio divina*, involving the whole person — mind, emotions, and body. Our book has suggested how you can best let photos speak to you, proposing a number of practical exercises. We have also looked at how photos can be used in groups, sharing some examples of how images can speak effectively in group settings. Finally, we have invited you to

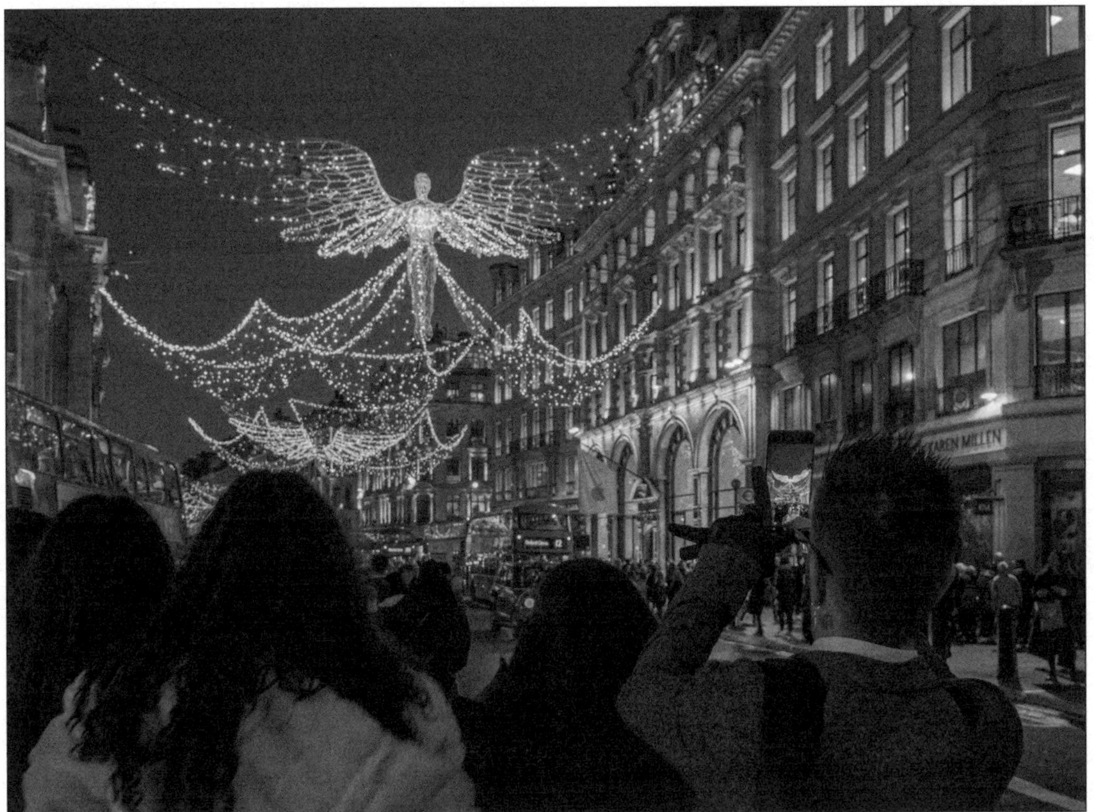

Entertaining Angels Unawares — Oxford Street, London © Stephen Radley

draw together your reflections in a personal photo journal, inspired by the ancient practice of keeping a 'Book of Hours'.

We are all different and we recognise some people will feel more drawn to some of the ideas we have shared than to others. Listen to who you are and draw on the parts of the book through which you find the most inspiration. We would also encourage you to try things which you might not feel as strongly drawn to, as moving outside our comfort zone can become a place of growth. Part of the beauty of co-authoring this book has been in our differences as authors: we have helped each other to see the world differently, as we have wrestled with the text, sharing the ideas which inspire us and which we each find helpful. When we started, we could not have predicted the outcome of this book and, like you, we continue to learn how to let photos speak. As elsewhere in life, we have learnt much as we have travelled this path. Part of our lifelong journey of learning has been writing this book, which we now offer to you.

Photos form a large part of modern life, and our aim within the pages of this book has been to inspire you to engage with your photos in different ways. Our hope is that you and your photography will continue to flourish, and through it you will see in ways which are filled with hope and wonder.

NOTES

1   The Bible: Exodus chapter 32.

2   duChemin, David (2018), *Everyone's A F*cking Photographer*. Available at: https://davidduchemin.com/2018/09/everyones-a-fcking-photographer/ [accessed 23 May 2022].

3   Richter, Philip J. (2017), *Spirituality in Photography: taking pictures with deeper vision* (London: Darton, Longman and Todd).

4   Merton, Thomas (1962), *New Seeds of Contemplation* (London: Burns and Oates), p.1.

5   Rohr, Richard, *What is Contemplation?*. Available at: https://cac.org/about/what-is-contemplation/ [accessed 5 November 2022].

6   Williams, Mark and Penman, Danny (2011), *Mindfulness: A Practical Guide to Finding Peace in a Frantic World* (London: Piatkus), p. x.

7   Stead, Tim (2016), *Mindfulness and Christian Spirituality: Making Space for God* (London: Society for Promoting Christian Knowledge).

8   Tyler, Peter (2018), *Christian Mindfulness: Theology and Practice* (London: SCM Press).

9   Williams, Mark and Penman, Danny (2011), *Mindfulness: A Practical Guide to Finding Peace in a Frantic World* (London: Piatkus), p.xi.

10 Stead, Tim (2016), *Mindfulness and Christian Spirituality: Making Space for God* (London: Society for Promoting Christian Knowledge), p. 6.

11 We are not able to recommend any courses. We understand one of the first places to offer training in mindfulness in the UK was the Oxford Mindfulness Foundation who collaborate with the University of Oxford's Department of Psychiatry. See https://www.oxfordmindfulness.org/about/ [accessed 5 December 2022].

12 Davey, Ruth, Look Again Photography Ltd, https://www.look-again.org/ [accessed 21 August 2022].

13 New Economics Foundation (2012), *Measuring Wellbeing: A Guide for Practitioners* (London: New Economics Foundation), p. 6.

14 See The University of Warwick: https://warwick.ac.uk/fac/sci/med/research/platform/wemwbs/ accessed 21/08/22

15 Aked, J., Marks, N. and Cordon, C. (2008), *A report presented to the Foresight Project on communicating the evidence base for improving people's well-being* (London: New Economics Foundation, available at: https://neweconomics.org/uploads/files/five-ways-to-wellbeing-1.pdf).

16 https://www.hopepublishing.com/find-hymns-hw/hw2996.aspx [accessed 6 December 2022].

17 Hooke, Kevin (2016), *A Dartmoor Psalter: Reflecting on the Psalms using Images of Dartmoor,* Blurb (no pagination).

18 Merton, Thomas, cited in Seitz, Ron (1995), *Song for Nobody: A Memory Vision of Thomas Merton* (Liguori, MO: Triumph Books), p. 133.

19 Perry, David (2017), *The Connexion*, 7, Winter/Spring, p.2: https://www.methodist.org.uk/media/4563/the-connexion-magazine-issue-7-050117.pdf [accessed 6 December 2022].

20 http://visualtheology.blogspot.co.uk/ [accessed 6 December 2022].

21 O'Neill, Gary, ed. and Shercliff, Liz, (2018), *Straw for the Bricks: Theological Reflection in Practice* (London: SCM Press), p. 10.

22 Education for Ministry Reading and Reflection Guide, Volume A, 2017–2018, p.52, http://www.stirlinganglican.org.au/wp/wp-content/uploads/2019/02/Education%20for%20Ministry%20vol.%20A%20for%202019.pdf [accessed 10/1/22].

23 Education for Ministry Reading and Reflection Guide, Volume A, 2017–2018, p.51.

24 Education for Ministry Reading and Reflection Guide, Volume A, 2017–2018, p.254.

25 Education for Ministry Reading and Reflection Guide, Volume A, 2017–2018, p.50.

26 17 November 2021, https://www.visualtheology.uk/blog/cop-out-26-valuing-our-precious-planet [accessed 11/1/22].

27 Magrassi, Mariano (1998), *Praying the Bible: An Introduction to Lectio Divina* (Collegeville, Minnesota: The Liturgical Press), p. 19.

28 Dysinger, Luke (1990), 'Accepting the Embrace of God: the ancient art of lectio divina', https://saintandrewsabbey.com/our-daily-life/accepting-the-embrace-of-god-the-ancient-art-of-lectio-divina/ [accessed 1/11/22].

29 Guigo II, trans. Edmund Colledge and James Walsh (1978), *The Ladder of Monks and Twelve Meditations* (London: Mowbray), p. 82.

30 Matthew 22:37.

31 John 16:22.

32 Matthew 9:4.

33 Van der Kolk, Bessel (2014), *The Body Keeps the Score: Brain, Mind, and Body in the healing of trauma* (New York: Penguin Books).

34 Elkins, James (2001), *Pictures and Tears : a history of people who have cried in front of paintings* (London: Routledge).

35 Smith, Rachel (2020), 'Visio Divina: History, Practice, and Resources' audio recording of workshop. Available at: https://worship.calvin.edu/resources/resource-library/visio-divina-history-practice-and-resources/ [accessed 23 September 2022].

36 *American Beauty* (1999), cited by IMDb https://www.imdb.com/title/tt0169547/characters/nm0004747 [accessed 6 December 2022].

37 https://labs.openai.com/ [accessed 6 December 2022].

38 https://www.theresekay.com/2021/02/03/vision-divina-part-3-an-example/ [accessed 10 November 2022].

39 Paintner, Christine, Valters (2013), *Eyes of the heart: photography as a Christian contemplative practice*. (Notre Dame, Indiana: Sorin Books).

40 'Praying with Art – Visio Divina', *Patheos*, 1 January 2000, https://www.patheos.com/resources/additional-resources/2000/01/pray-with-art – excerpts reproduced by kind permission of Tim Mooney. The stages are simply numbered – we have added our own titles.

41 'Praying with "Migrant Mother" using Visio Divina', 24 February 2011, https://spiritualdrawingboard.com/2011/02/24/praying-with-migrant-mother-using-visio-divina/ – excerpts reproduced by kind permission of Julie McCarty.

42 Phillips, Jan (2000), *God is at Eye Level: Photography as a Healing Art* (Wheaton, Illinois: Quest Books Theosophical Pub. House).

43 Warner, Meg (2020), *Joseph A Story of Resilience* (London: SPCK).

44 Puchalski, Christina, M; Vitillo, Robert; Hull, Sharon, K.; and Reller, Nancy (2014), 'Improving the Spiritual Dimension of Whole Person Care: Reaching National and International Consensus', *Journal of Palliative Medicine*, 17 (6) pp.642–656. available at: https://www.ncbi.nlm.nih.gov/pmc/articles/PMC4038982/ [accessed 15 July2022]

45 Weiser, Judy (1999), *Photo Therapy techniques exploring the secrets of personal snapshots and family albums: phototherapy techniques* (Vancouver: Phototherapy Center Publishers), p. 1.

46 Zajonc, Arthur (1993), *Catching the Light: The Entwined History of Light and Mind* (Oxford: Oxford University Press).

47 The Bible, Genesis 9:13-16.

48 Schipperges, Heinrich (1997), *Hildegard of Bingen: Healing and the Nature of the Cosmos* (Princeton, NJ: Markus Wiener), p. 66.

49 Cited in Fox, Matthew (2000/1983), *Original Blessing* (New York: Jeremy P. Tarcher/ Putnam). p. 68.

50 Birren, Faber (1978), *Color Psychology and Color Therapy* (Secaucus, NJ: Citadel), p. 169.

51 St Clair, Kassia (2018), *The Secret Lives of Colour* (London: John Murray), p.180.

52 Simone Weil (1959), *Waiting on God* (London: Fontana), p. 120.

53 Hopkins, Gerard Manley (1970), 'To What Serves Mortal Beauty?', in *Poems*, 4th ed. (Oxford: Oxford University Press), no.62, p. 98.

54 Gernsheim, Helmut and Alison (1965), *A Concise History of Photography* (London: Thames and Hudson), p. 191.

55 Thiessen, Gesa E. (2004), *Theological Aesthetics: A Reader* (London: SCM Press), p. 6.

56 Viladesau, Richard (2006), *The Beauty of the Cross: The Passion of Christ in Theology and the Arts, from the catacombs to the eve of the Renaissance* (Oxford: Oxford University Press), pp. 9, 12.

57 Tedeschi, Richard G.; Shakespeare-Finch, Jane; Taku, Kanako; and Calhoun, Laurence G. (2018), *Posttraumatic Growth: Theory, Research and Applications* (London: Routledge).

58 Eco, Umberto and McEwan, Alastair (trans). (2010), *On Beauty: A History of a Western Idea* (London: MacLehose).

59 Eco, Umberto and McEwan, Alastair (trans) (2010). *On Beauty: A History of a Western Idea* (London: MacLehose), p. 41.

60 Eco, Umberto and McEwan, Alastair (trans) (2010), *On Beauty: A History of a Western Idea* (London: MacLehose), p. 48.

61 Bianchi, Enzo (2015), *Lectio Divina: From God's Word to our Lives* (London: SPCK), p. 84.

62 Paintner, C. Valters (2013), *Eyes of the Heart: Photography as a Christian Contemplative Practice* (Notre Dame, Indiana: Sorin Books), p. 13.

63 Picoult, J. (2018), *Small Great Things* (New York: Ballantine Books), p.19.

64 Hirsch, Alan (2017), *5Q: Reactivating the Original Intelligence and Capacity of the Body of Christ* (Cody, Wyoming: 100M).

65 Goldsmith, Malcolm and Wharton, Martin (1993), *Knowing Me, Knowing You: Exploring Personality Type and Temperament* (London: SPCK), pp. 156-181.

66 Goldsmith, Malcolm and Wharton, Martin (1993), *Knowing Me, Knowing You: Exploring Personality Type and Temperament* (London: SPCK), pp. 20-22.

67 'How do I know if I'm a Sensor or Intuitive? What's my personality? (MBTI)', Willow Tree Training and Professional Development video, https://youtu.be/t3y0BuHJoFo [accessed 8 December 2022].

68 Goldsmith, Malcolm and Wharton, Martin (1993), *Knowing Me, Knowing You: Exploring Personality Type and Temperament* (London: SPCK), p. 136. Of 300 mainstream Anglican Laity 77 per cent were Feelers. This figure is broadly in line with Andy's experience in Methodist churches.

69 https://www.16personalities.com/country-profiles/united-kingdom [accessed 8 December 2022].

70 Baker, Jonny (2021), *Pioneer Practice* (GETSidetracked), p. 106.

71 See, for example, Peter and Cornelius's dreams and encounter with each other in Acts 10:1-38.

72 Goldsmith, Malcolm and Wharton, Martin (1993), *Knowing Me, Knowing You: Exploring Personality Type and Temperament* (London: SPCK), p. 37 – technically this is the opposite of our second most dominant characteristic.

73 https://pres-outlook.org/2016/01/through-the-lens-photography-connects-community-with-god/ [accessed 8 December 2022].

74 Eshleman, Stephen F. Obold and Perez, Shelley E. Varner (2021) 'I Don't Do Religion: Using Nature Photographs to Engage Patients in Spiritual Reflection', *Journal of Pain and Symptom Management*, 64 (5), p. 306.

75 Eshleman, Stephen F. Obold and Perez, Shelley E. Varner (2021), 'I Don't Do Religion: Using Nature Photographs to Engage Patients in Spiritual Reflection', *Journal of Pain and Symptom Management*, 64 (5), p. 306.

76 Eshleman, Stephen F. Obold and Perez, Shelley E. Varner (2021), 'I Don't Do Religion: Using Nature Photographs to Engage Patients in Spiritual Reflection', *Journal of Pain and Symptom Management*, 64 (5), p. 307.

77 Eshleman, Stephen F. Obold and Perez, Shelley E. Varner (2021), 'I Don't Do Religion: Using Nature Photographs to Engage Patients in Spiritual Reflection', *Journal of Pain and Symptom Management*, 64 (5), p. 307.

78 It is advisable to independently check the copyright of any images. We also recommend www.pexels.com and www.unsplash.com.

79 https://www.kairosmovement.org.uk/divine-focus/ [accessed 8 December 2022].

80 See, for example: https://www.methodist.org.uk/media/5027/dd-explore-devotion-keeping-a-spiritual-journal-0313.pdf [accessed 8 December 2022].

81 Generic term for data storage that is hosted by large companies, but accessible via the internet.

82 https://jonnybaker.blogs.com/jonnybaker/2018/09/give-me-eyes-to-see-like-a-photographer.html [accessed 8 December 2022].

83 Richter, Philip J. (2017), *Spirituality in Photography: Taking Pictures with Deeper Vision* (London: Darton, Longman and Todd).

84 Lewis, Clive, S. (1950/2009), *The Lion, the Witch and the Wardrobe* (London: HarperCollins Children's Books), p. 88.

85 Roger S. Wieck (1997), *Painted Prayers: The Book of Hours in Medieval and Renaissance Art* (New York: George Braziller).